The HEArt solutions to anger
Howard Lipke as he helped tra
having anger attacks. The tools are profoundly apt, helping the individual prepare for sensitive situations and providing cognitive, emotional, and physiological mechanisms to deal with those situations. The result is a HEArt-prepared individual who is not easily triggered into anger. This system works; anyone prone to angry outbursts should read this book.

Don R. Catherall, Ph.D.
Editor, Handbook of Stress, Trauma, and the Family
(2004, Routledge)

Drawing upon over 30 years of experience working with military veterans from all eras, Dr. Lipke has written the most comprehensive and practical clinical guide available on understanding, preventing, and managing post-traumatic anger. After introducing the Hidden Emotion Articulation (HEArt) program developed and clinically tested within the VA, Lipke provides straightforward explanations and meaningful examples of the nature, causes, and prevention of destructive anger, written in everyday language so that both clinicians and clients can immediately apply lessons learned. Well-designed "real-world" exercises are presented to help clients learn effective ways to control their anger before it controls them. This book is a "must have" for all helping professionals and clients coping with traumatic stress injuries, particularly members of the warrior class including active-duty military, veterans, law enforcement, journalists, and family members.

Mark C. Russell, Ph.D., ABPP
Commander, U.S. Navy (Retired)
Director, Institute of War Stress Injuries and Social Justice,
Antioch University Seattle

As a clinical psychologist at the Captain James A. Lovell Federal Health Care Center (formerly the North Chicago VA Medical Center) Dr. Lipke developed the HEArt program for service members and veterans with histories of post-traumatic stress disorder (PTSD). It focuses on potentially destructive anger and examination of underlying emotions that one's anger may be protecting against. The HEArt program has become a key aspectz of the clinical programming on the residential PTSD unit and is a strong tool for anybody recovering from the effects of PTSD.

Anthony R. Peterson, Psy.D.
Section Chief, PTSD Programs
Captain James A. Lovell Federal Health Care Center,
North Chicago, IL

Based on clinical observation and excellent scholarship, Dr. Lipke's HEArt program fills the need for an easy-to-follow guide for understanding and managing destructive anger. Looking at anger's cognitive and emotional underpinnings, it is wonderfully written, clear, and organized, breaking anger down into manageable bites. While it is initially directed toward a veteran audience, this program would be helpful for just about everyone, including therapy groups, graduate students, and mental health professionals. It is easy to understand, a pleasure to read, and I highly recommend it!

Carolyn V. Edwards, Ph.D.
Roosevelt University, Chicago, IL

In the spring of 2012, Dr. Howard Lipke presented the core concepts of the HEArt program to 20 high school students in an evening program for [those] who have already dropped out of high school or who are at risk of dropping out. The socioeconomic and emotional issues these students face create an environment of fear, frustration and anger. Often these tensions erupt in violent behavior.

The presentation gave them a way of looking beyond their circumstances to ways in which they could understand their own responses to the environment. Telling an edgy group of teenagers to look for the fear behind their anger took a fair amount of courage. Of course their adolescent bravado and school-of-hard-knocks training made them resist the idea that they could be afraid of anything. With patient persistence, engaging anecdotes and clarifying diagrams, Dr. Lipke explained the link between fear and anger. He gave them some real insight into their behavior. Indeed, for the remainder of the semester the students applied the HEArt paradigm to the fictional characters we encountered. They began to see the truth in the correlation between these emotions, and hopefully could begin to apply this insight to their own behavior.

I believe his program is extremely valuable for troubled adolescents. They are struggling to understand why their lives are so chaotic and how they can make them better. Giving young people real tools for behavior analysis is key to raising conscious, caring, fully functioning adults. I recommend the program with enthusiasm.

June A. Kramer
Teacher, Barrington High School, Barrington, IL

Don't I Have the Right to Be Angry?

Don't I Have the Right to Be Angry?
The HEArt Program for Veterans and Others Who Want to Prevent Destructive Anger

Howard Lipke, Ph.D.

published by Good Looking Software, Inc.

Published by Good Looking Software, Inc.
1078 Pear Tree Ln., Wheeling, IL 60090
www.GoodLookingSoftware.com

To download and print worksheets, figures, supplemental materials, and errata from the book, visit:

www.HowardLipke.com/DontIHaveARightToBeAngry
www.GoodLookingSoftware.com/DontIHaveARightToBeAngry

First Published, 2013

PREFACE

This work should not be reprinted without the express permission of Howard Lipke.

This book was written for professional counselors in the mental health field, veterans and members of the general public who wish to better understand emotion — anger in particular — and perhaps work to prevent destructive anger.

This book differs from many anger related books by emphasizing anger as a defense against other emotions over other important ways of affecting anger.

Although most sections describe the HEArt program in general, others are intended especially for counselors and veterans.

Any time you engage in activity that touches on important aspects of life, you may react with unexpected emotions, including pain. So the choice is to try to avoid the issues addressed below or to learn about them and yourself. I hope you find what is written below helpful, but if it awakens emotional reactions which you find difficult to manage, or need help to fully explore, please seek the assistance of a licensed professional.

DEDICATION

To my wife Lynn. If Tolstoy is right about happy families, then there are some other very lucky people out there.

ACKNOWLEDGEMENTS

I find writing this section of a book the most difficult. There are many people who helped both directly and indirectly and I don't like the idea of missing anyone. I apologize and ask forgiveness in advance for people accidentally left out. While I recognize the help of those thanked, it is not their fault if there is anything in here that isn't as sensible as I think. They, obviously, cannot be held responsible for how I interpreted and expressed their suggestions.

There are lots and lots of people who have helped develop the HEArt program and this book. It is ironic, but common, for a therapist's greatest debt to be to those he tried to help. In my case it is the veterans I have known and worked with to try to limit the damage of war, and to make the most of their considerable potential. I became a psychologist partly to try to more fully understand the general human experience, mine included. To the extent that I have done so, much of the credit goes to veterans for their willingness to share their experiences, thoughts and feelings relating to the most extreme of human conditions. I cannot mention any names because of confidentiality concerns.

I also thank my fellow mental health professionals. Most of them have been on staff at what was called the North Chicago VA Medical Center, and is now the Captain James A. Lovell Federal Health Care Center. In particular, I want to mention staff and interns from the psychology department there, as well as the Stress Disorder Treatment Unit (SDTU). Orv Lips (who taught me a model for combining education and counseling that allowed this work to develop), Karen Paddock, John Schaut, Sheila Perrin, Al Botkin, Sumner Garte, Jim Moore, Edith Taber, and Anthony Peterson must be mentioned. Neysa Etienne, Julia Smith, and Brandi Booth, now doctors, were very helpful in the development of these materials and ideas when they were interns.

I also thank Francine Shapiro, who taught me EMDR which allowed me to more fully understand the relationship between the past and the present, and to see a new path to healing. I thank Drs. William Zangwill, Jim Talbert, and Tim Hull for their friendship and willingness to consider and discuss these ideas. I thank Dr. Charles Figley, whose encouragement and example have inspired me and many others.

I thank my wife Lynn, who helped tremendously with editing for clarity and providing wonderfully patient support. If there are failures in clarity, I still marvel at how much she did to improve the work. I thank my daughter Nora for her discussion and support, and my son Aaron Surrain, who helped with clarifying ideas, and especially with the graphics and production. Jonathan Houghton and Aaron helped with the final editing and development, which allowed this to be published at all. I also thank other members of my family and my friends for their support, love, and friendship throughout the years.

TABLE OF CONTENTS

CHAPTER I:
INTRODUCTION

Perhaps you have heard, or even said: "Don't I have the right to be angry?" as if the anger is something to be cherished. But now, maybe, you have some doubts about the amount and intensity of anger that it makes sense to claim.

The HEArt program offers four levels of psychological recommendations to people trying to eliminate problems with destructive anger. Each level is valuable in its own way. The beginning levels focus on the immediate safety of everyone in the anger situation. The later levels seek to prevent destructive anger from even becoming an issue. All of the suggestions are based on established principles of human learning and behavior. Most have been part of human knowledge for centuries and the standard practice of psychology for decades, with a few important additions and changes in emphasis. There is nothing offered here which I myself have not found personally useful as I have attempted to navigate the common challenges of life.

Some of the principles below you may have already heard or thought of yourself. But it may not hurt to hear some of this again. As the old saying goes, "We need to remember more than we need to learn."

1.1: AN OVERVIEW OF FOUR LEVELS OF SKILLS

I

Physical Presence
Removing yourself from dangerous anger situations

In this level, we learn to recognize and stay away from, or get away from, situations that have a good chance of leading to destructive anger. This method is sometimes looked down upon as copping out or ducking the problem. However, for the people who have most often used this program — combat veterans — this first skill level is sometimes a life-or-death proposition. For the rest of us as well, sometimes it's best to just walk, or even run, away.

II

Physiological Control
Be calm, breathe, count to 10

This level is attained by learning to reduce the bodily feelings of anger through calming exercises or meditation, distracting mental images, or distracting thinking (counting to 10). Anger, like all emotions, includes both physical sensations and thoughts. We believe someone has hurt us, and can sometimes feel the anger in our body: in our heart rate, on our face, in our muscles. As we feel the anger build in our body, our thoughts of anger increase. If we can learn to calm our body, sometimes our thoughts calm, the cycle is broken, and the anger decreases. You may notice I didn't use the word "relax." That is because some people, including many veterans, believe that to be relaxed is to be in danger. However, all would probably agree that there are levels of excitement or arousal that make situations more dangerous than safe. Like any skill, the exercises considered at this level must be practiced, so that they are available in the situations when you most need them.

III
Thinking Rationally
Does it make sense?

This level consists of learning that our opinion of the meaning of events has much to do with our emotional reaction. For example, if we focus on the assumption that the person cutting us off in traffic thinks he is getting over on us, and this means he thinks we are a chump, then we will get angry. Our response may be different if we consider one or more of the following:

- The other driver simply made a mistake.
- The mistake might have been made by someone upset about a crisis.
- Our desire to "teach them a lesson" might hurt innocent bystanders, which we will regret more than letting someone slide for cutting us off.
- We have done this to others accidentally, and most of them did not come after us.
- Etc.

The other aspect of thinking rationally is to consider if our angry reaction is not an overreaction, even if the person is really thinking he is getting over on us. Is it worth it? You may be surprised to find that spiritual beliefs are part of this level (see Chapter 5.5).

IV
Identifying the Emotion Beneath the Anger
What emotion could the anger be hiding?

The highest level — the "heart" of the HEArt program — is the most difficult to explain, though potentially the most valuable. This level is based on the idea that, like all emotions, anger — even destructive anger — has an activity or a behavior that goes with it. For anger, the activity is getting rid of something, just as the activity that goes with fear is getting away or hiding. In the case of anger, sometimes the activity is not getting rid of an external threat, like an enemy, but rather getting rid of, or blocking, a painful emotion like terror or grief. When we practice naming that hidden, painful emotion, the anger loses its job of hiding the emotion. It doesn't come up as strongly, and sometimes doesn't come up at all. Therefore, it doesn't have to be managed or controlled.

HEArt stands for Hidden Emotion Articulation — that is, finding and naming the hidden emotion.

1.2: STRUCTURE OF THE BOOK

Before we get to the details of the HEArt program, I would like to briefly discuss the structure of this book, which is a little different than many similar books. After some discussion of anger and emotion in general, it will move directly to the most advanced level of the program. There are several reasons for this: The earlier skills (Levels I, II, III), while of sometimes life-saving importance, are known to many people, are fairly easy to understand, and have already been tried by most people.

The overall HEArt project might be compared to getting your Ph.D. in the prevention of destructive anger. Level I would be like an associate's degree, II a bachelor's degree, III a master's, and IV a Ph.D. Each level teaches useful material, and sometimes even the Level I knowledge, though not as complex as what comes later, is what is necessary for a situation, no matter how far you have gone in your education. As you will see, I try to make the case that if you learn to practice the level IV skills well, the earlier skills, especially Level I, will not be as necessary.

As I mentioned earlier, this book is structured for multiple audiences. Those interested in the parts directly about anger prevention can easily identify and read just those sections; similarly, veterans or mental health professionals interested in background information can locate those sections as well.

Although simply knowing these ideas may help, practicing them will help more. To that end, I've included practice exercises throughout.

It seems to be a basic truth that, in the vast majority of attempts at change, practice and persistence are the majority of the battle. Thomas Edison has been quoted as making the statement that genius is "one percent inspiration and 99 percent perspiration," and though I'm hoping that these ideas will carry more than one percent of the benefit here, I don't think I want to argue with Edison on this one.

1.3: MY EXPERIENCE WITH VETERANS

The concepts in this book have been presented to veterans as part of a comprehensive treatment program for combat-related posttraumatic stress disorder (PTSD). PTSD is an official medical diagnostic category; that is one truth. Another truth, which I also emphasize to my clients, is that combat and preparation for combat involve learning. In combat, behavior and reaction patterns change to those that are necessary to increase chances of survival there, though they may have the opposite effect in non-combat situations. One of the learned changes has to do with emotion.

The concepts discussed below are as much about emotion learning as about PTSD. This is not to say that biological changes do not also occur in PTSD. However, all life experiences include biological changes, including learning to decrease undesired destructive anger.

While people need to decide for themselves what they would like help with, I do sometimes provide some information to clarify the decision. I have often cited an observation made in a radio interview by Dexter Filkins, at the time a *New York Times* reporter who had been embedded with the U.S. Marines in the battle for Fallujah, Iraq. In discussing why soldiers did not express their grief in the field, he said the answer was obvious: it was a luxury that couldn't be afforded then. Their mindset, he said, was "I'll deal with it when I get home."

During more than 30 years as a VA psychologist, working most often with combat veterans, my job has been to help those who got home and then, for many powerful reasons, still didn't "deal with it." In this effort to help combat survivors, some other basic questions, which may seem obvious to outsiders but were not to the veterans themselves, have had to be addressed. The first: What is the "it" that has to be dealt with? In Filkins' example, "it" is, at the very least, the grief of the loss of a friend, and maybe additionally, the horror of seeing the effects of weapons on human bodies, as well as the pervasive, if hidden, fear in combat situations. (I heard one Iraq War veteran say that he didn't exhale until he got home.) All that doesn't even take into account the guilt feelings (based on a false concept of human nature) that often occur because one has survived, or has not been visibly wounded severely enough to justify the amount of mental pain.

If not during the combat deployment, then after getting out, the "it" might change, and become not just the immediate grief, but also nightmares, flashbacks, pervasive thoughts of combat situations, startle responses, rage, emotional numbness, social isolation, depression, and other symptoms of posttraumatic stress disorder (PTSD). If you read on, you will see one proposal of how all of the above may be related to destructive anger/rage.

One of the reasons veterans often give for not taking the time to get help is that they consider it selfish to do so; they say they are not comfortable getting help, only helping others. On occasion I have asked them to consider the cards on airplanes that tell passengers what to do if the breathing masks drop down. The cards instruct passengers to put their own mask on before helping a child to put his mask on. Getting the help you need is not unlike putting your mask on first.

1.4: HEART, ANGER, AND PTSD

While the ideas in this book were developed through work with people who had problems connected to PTSD, it is not explicitly about PTSD. In general, I think people can have some but not all of the PTSD symptoms as part of their reaction to trauma. They may have other problems as well, such as depression or phobias. These may be seen as more interrelated than is commonly discussed.

In the various official diagnostic manuals of mental health problems, there have been various systems for describing the symptoms of PTSD. They almost always include: re-experiencing (nightmares, flashbacks), avoidance (physically avoiding reminders of trauma), emotional numbing, and hyperarousal (anger, anxiety).

If anger has its root in fear, and fear is part of the partial flashback experience, then re-experiencing and hyperarousal are clearly connected. If physical avoidance is partly to prevent an anger reaction, then avoidance and hyperarousal are also connected. Further, if anger is to protect from painful emotions when emotional numbing is ineffective, then that aspect of avoidance and hyperarousal are connected too.

Given these interconnections, it seems possible that if none of the problems occur in isolation, then addressing one of the problems will affect the others. Based on the above analysis of the connection, destructive anger may be a good place to start.

CHAPTER II:
ANGER AND OTHER EMOTION
FAMILIES

2.1: ANGER AND ITS JOB, AND DEFINING DESTRUCTIVE ANGER

Anger is the name of a family of emotions ranging in intensity from rage down to irritation or frustration. Anger is a basic emotion. We are born with the capacity for it; it has a biology, behavior associated with it and a job. Its job is to push things away, to get rid of them, even to destroy them.

People have a mixed relationship with anger. In some situations, it is something to be respected, or even a requirement.[1] In other situations, it is considered a problem, or even a sin. Sometimes anger will save us, or at least give us the energy to improve things. But when anger is used inappropriately, in the wrong place or with too much intensity, it can be destructive to us, our best goals and those we care about.

Many veterans have told me they don't ever get angry, they only get enraged. I think it will be helpful to consider rage the extreme version of an anger emotion.

This book distinguishes between helpful, appropriate anger and destructive anger. HEArt focuses on understanding the nature of destructive anger, then using that understanding to prevent or diminish it and its negative effects in ourselves and, maybe,

---

1   There are times in combat, as will be discussed, in which anger or rage can save one from an impossible situation, but more commonly, there are times where manageable levels of anger will help motivate one to important action, or when failure to show some sympathetic anger concerning a friend who has been wronged will be seen as a lack of caring. (Even if you know that worry is the root of the anger, it will still be genuine.)

in others. Each person must decide for himself or herself what is appropriate anger.

Consider these words from Aristotle: "Now he who is angry at what and with whom he ought, and further, in right manner and time, and for proper length of time, is praised."

2.2: ANGER AND FEAR

When we think about anger as having the job of attacking, to try to get rid of people or things, the question arises: Why are we bothering to get rid of them? The most obvious answer is that they are somehow a threat. If they are a threat, wouldn't it be more logical to first have the emotion of fear — the emotion connected with hiding or getting away from a threat — rather than anger? If so, then perhaps the anger arises to make sure we don't feel fear. (It should also be mentioned that people who have been in terrifying, traumatic situations might have their fear closer to the surface, so the anger is always near the surface to block it.)

Now, if the anger will help us effectively fight what we fear, as in some especially desperate situations, then it makes sense. But it doesn't make sense if anger blocks the signals fear gives us to identify the actual nature of the threat and find the most effective way to overcome it, if it truly is a threat.

2.3: BACKGROUND: RECENT HISTORY OF THE IDEA OF ANGER BLOCKING OTHER EMOTION

I am not the first person to examine this idea. The psychiatrist Harry Stack Sullivan wrote in 1954:

> ...Anger is much more pleasant to experience than anxiety. The brute facts are that it is much more comfortable to feel angry than anxious. Admitting that neither is too delightful, there is everything in favor of anger. Anger

*often leaves one sort of worn out, and one thing and an-
other, very often makes things worse in the long run, but
there is a curious feeling of power when one is angry. In
other words, the expressive pattern of anger tends to drive
things away. Not only is anxiety thus avoided, but the
initial index of its presence fades from observation, and
you are left with no clear idea of how this all came about.
In somewhere around 94 percent of all occasions on which
you are anxious, the security operations called out by that
anxiety are the things you are perfectly clear on, whereas
the precipitating anxiety is observed. (p. 109)*

In his 1958 novel *Things Fall Apart*, African author Chinua
Achebe examined the roots of anger in the book's protagonist,
Okonkwo:

*Okonkwo ruled his household with a heavy hand. His
wives, especially his youngest, live in perpetual fear of
his fiery temper, and so did his little children. Perhaps
down in his heart Okonkwo was not a cruel man. But
his whole life was dominated by fear, the fear of failure
and of weakness. It was deeper and more intimate than
the fear of evil and capricious gods and of magic, the fear
of the forest, and of the forces of nature, malevolent, red
in tooth and claw. Okonkwo's fear was greater than these.
It was not external but lay deep within himself. It was
the fear of himself, lest he should be found to resemble
his father. Even as a little boy he had resented his father's
failure and weakness, and even now he still remembered
how he had suffered when a playmate had told him that
his father was agbala. That is how Okonkwo first came
to know that agbala was not only another name for a
woman, it could also mean a man who had taken no
title. And so his father Unoka had loved. One of those
things was a gentleness and another was idleness. (p. 13)*

2.4: BACKGROUND FOR VETERANS: HISTORY OF ANGER AND FEAR IN RELATION TO COMBAT

These ideas are quite a bit older than the 1950s, especially in connection with war. In Virgil's epic poem the *Aeneid*, after the city of Troy is destroyed, the hero Aeneas is about to focus on taking revenge when his mother, the goddess Venus, intervenes. Here the emotion being blocked is not fear, but grief:

> *What joy, to glut my heart with the fires of vengence, bring some peace to the ashes of my people. Whirling words — I was swept away by fury now when all of a sudden there my loving mother stood before my eyes, but I had never seen her more clearly, her pure radiance shining down upon me through the night, the goddess in all her glory, just as the gods behold her build, her awesome beauty. Grasping my hand she held me back, adding this from her rose-red lips: "My son, what grief could incite such blazing anger? Why such fury? And the love you bore for me once where has it gone? Why don't you look first to where you left your father, Anchiese, spent with age? Do your wife Creusa, and son Ascanius still survive?" (p. 95)*

In Shakespeare's Macbeth, the character Malcolm uses his understanding of the relationship among emotions to manipulate another character, the grieving Macduff, into attacking Macbeth.

> *"Be comforted,*
> *Let's make us md'cines of our great revenge*
> *To cure this deadly grief."*

Later he adds:

> *"Be this the whetstone of your sword.*
> *Let grief*
> *Convert to anger; blunt not the heart, enrage it." (Act III, Sc. 3)*

2.5: A FICTIONAL EXAMPLE: SAM AND JOE

Consider this situation: Joe threatens to lie about Sam to their supervisor, and Sam reacts with rage. Hidden by Sam's rage may be fear or worry about one or many things, each of which would require a different effective response:

- Sam will lose his job.
- Sam will look bad and lose his self-esteem.
- Sam will look bad and lose the respect of others.
- Since Joe is wrong, Sam will lose his belief that things are fair.
- Sam will have to waste time dealing with this, keeping him from getting other work done.
- If Sam thought Joe was a friend, he may have lost Joe's friendship. Because this behavior is so out of character for Joe, it may also be a sign that something is seriously wrong with Joe.

Does Sam have a right to be angry? Does it matter, and will it do him any good? Maybe, maybe not.

Sam may not be motivated to change his anger if it's effective at getting him get what he wants — for example, scaring Joe so that he doesn't talk. If that is the case, what is being offered here will be of little value to Sam, though it may help people who know him understand what is going on under the surface.

I hope it is clear by now that understanding anger's underlying emotions doesn't decrease the anger by itself. Knowing that fear is being hidden by anger is usually just the first step to using rational thought to address that fear. If, in the example of Sam, he realizes that his anger masks the fear of losing the respect of others or his own self-esteem, then he can rationally consider whether or not it makes sense to base his self-esteem on Joe's opinion. As you might see, he is using the Level IV skill to get to the Level III skill quickly and directly.

2.6: TIME FOR A WARNING

It is important to be careful with how you use this knowledge. If you go around telling angry people that under their anger is some kind of fear or pain, this knowledge is likely to increase their hidden fear, requiring more anger to block it. An even worse idea is to tell these people you know exactly what their fear is about, because when you get to the particular, there is a very good chance you will be wrong about the specific thing they fear.

2.7: BACKGROUND: SELF-ESTEEM

Since anger is sometimes related to the fear of losing self-esteem, this may be a good time to share some thoughts about self-esteem. Our self-esteem is the judgment we make of our own worth. High self-esteem is conventionally considered good and low self-esteem bad.

Instead of worrying about self-esteem, a better alternative may be to try to understand why things happen to us and what we can do to change our situation. There is considerable research and discussion in the mental health field about "self-focused attention" and how it is related to psychological problems.

Defending our character to ourselves and others, establishing that we are good or strong, is much like using anger to cover fear. In both situations, we avoid the work of identifying and addressing the root of the problem, which is much more difficult. It's like a baseball player continually evaluating his stats, comparing them to those of his teammates, instead of putting in the hours of practice that will actually improve his skills.

In the example of Sam, if he understands that his anger at Joe masks the fear of losing his self-esteem, and recognizes that the question of self-esteem is a diversion, then he can decrease his anger to a non-destructive level as he responds to Joe.

Self-esteem is tricky in some other ways. Sometimes a client will complain that he has low self-esteem and wants to improve it.

Depending on the situation and the quality of our relationship, we may have the following exchange:

> Me: Does this mean you think you are something like a worthless person?
>
> Client: Yes.
>
> Me: I don't agree. We've talked a while and I think you are a plenty valuable person. Don't you agree?
>
> Client: No, not really.
>
> Me: Then where do you get the nerve to disagree with me about a person's worth? I am a professional expert in the field, yet you disagree. I hardly call that low self-esteem.

Almost everyone believes that they are their own best judge. So if we are to consider self-esteem at all, it might be best to consider how good we are at very specific things, in very specific circumstances, which also can lead us down the path to improvement.

Exception No. 1

Having said all this, self-esteem, like anger, is something we cannot, and maybe should not, try to completely get rid of. In the same way that anger can keep us motivated, particularly in life-or-death situations where it may be needed to overcome potentially paralyzing fear, there are times when we may want and need to use self-esteem. We mobilize all our resources and ask the question (if I can be forgiven the archaic use of gender) "Am I a man or a mouse?" to motivate us to deal with important challenges.

Lest self-esteem and anger only be thought of as being motivating in combat, it is important to point out that anger and self-esteem can also help us refrain from attacking when that is the right and courageous thing to do.

When you have a debate within yourself about self-esteem, who exactly is doing the attacking, who is defending and who is determining the winner?

Exception No. 2

It must be recognized that, for some people, low self-esteem doesn't have to do with negative self-judgment, but rather learned emotional reactions. When a person finds himself or herself overwhelmed by negative emotion while facing potential social criticism, or physical challenges that are not dangerously outside one's capabilities, this learned feeling reaction might be near what one might reasonably consider low self-esteem. But in that case, using this term, which strongly implies judgment, is more distracting than helpful. (Chapter 3.6 will further address this learned, memory-based feeling reaction.)

2.8: BACKGROUND FOR MENTAL HEALTH PROFESSIONALS: FEAR, SHAME, AND GUILT

Fear, like anger, encompasses a wide range of emotions. The fear family ranges from terror to trepidation and also includes shame and guilt. Shame is the fear of what others might think of us, while guilt, which is often thought of as similar to shame, is more like anger at the self.

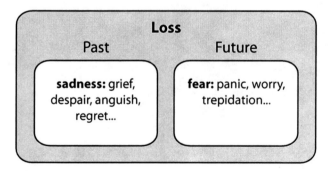

Figure 1

Some therapists who see shame as the root of many psychological problems may object to discussing it as one of the fear emotions. I agree that shame is important to focus on in the counseling process, but I think identifying the specific fears it represents is crucial to understanding it.

The relationship between fear and shame has been previously discussed by learning theorists Dollard and Miller (1950): "We may speculate that many socially learned drives, such as guilt, suspicion, shame, pride, the need for social conformity ... are composed to a considerable extent of fear" (p. 90). Tangney and Dearing (2002) also discuss the relationship among shame, guilt, and anger, and cite the work of psychologists who have preceded them, particularly H.B. Lewis, who inspires much of their work. Following Lewis, they propose the chief distinction between shame and guilt is that shame is about the self, and guilt is about the deed. They go on to discuss the defensive anger associated with shame. They also, based on their research, conclude that shame has characteristics like fear, such as the desire to hide or escape, and concern about the evaluation of others. Guilt has attributes common with anger, such as being less painful than shame, and being associated with taking corrective action.

When guilt blocks fear, it eventually becomes intolerable. The person may then shift to finding a way to blame (and be angry at) others, which also becomes unsustainable after a while (because there is often too much evidence that they're not totally to blame and/or it is clear the anger is too great or self-destructive). Then the anger turns back into guilt, starting the cycle anew.

Figure 2

While I agree that guilt (self-anger, as I have it) can function as a defense because it is preferred to shame (fear), I think they underestimate how painful guilt can be, perhaps because their research does not much consider guilt associated with extremes such as combat situations.

2.9: BACKGROUND FOR MENTAL HEALTH PROFESSIONALS: MORE ON ANGER AS GUILT

A common belief of psychologists is that guilt is anger at others turned inward (Tavis, 1989). While I agree that guilt is anger turned inward, I believe that it is there to block internal sadness/fear before those emotions can be felt, or at least fully felt. Just as shame is a specific form of fear, I think guilt is a specific form of anger aimed at the self. Since guilt is a very powerfully negative feeling, it doesn't seem possible that it would exist as some kind of protection against feeling bad. I will attempt to make the case that as bad as guilt is, we sometimes choose it over sadness or fear.

To understand this point, we must first look at our self-identity and how it relates to our understanding of the world. We all have basic ideas of reality, and who we are, that not only determine much of what we do or say, but also what we see and hear. (Think of the times you have misheard something to be what you expected, not what was said, or mistook a stranger for someone you knew.) Some of these patterns of understanding start when we are children, and some start later. Sometimes they are imprinted by repeated experiences, and sometimes through brief, powerful experiences, such as a traumatic event. It should also be mentioned that learning to define the world and ourselves occurs not just through punishment and trauma, but also through positive experiences and rewards.

We all define ourselves in many ways: as men or women, as members of nations, religious or ethnic groups, schools, military organizations, etc. We all have some awareness of the cost of losing any of these identities. When we act outside the rules of any of these identities, we are punished, sometimes harshly. So if a boy is punished for crying, he is reminded —whether or not it is true — that to not cry is a choice he can make, and that not crying is part of retaining his identity. So in a sense, punishment tells us that we still have an identity, that we haven't yet lost it. If we lose it, however, sadness is an appropriate emotion. Another would be fear of the consequences of losing it.

Guilt can be seen as the self-punishing signal that an identity has not been lost. Two things are then protected: our membership in the group (our role), and the fact that the group is still what we think it is and worth being a member of, which means the world has not changed. This may or may not be a correct signal. It may be that others have seen us as losing our identity, but what matters to the guilt-feeling person is that we don't see our identity as lost, so the sadness is avoided.

The power of maintaining identity can be seen when people choose to end their lives rather than lose their role in their families or in society. Perhaps the reports of suicide after the stock market crash of 1929 make sense when viewed as a choice to lose life itself rather than accept the sadness and fear that accompany the loss of these peoples' roles as wealthy, successful businessmen.

Accepting martyrdom to achieve a reward in the afterlife is not the same thing. From the point of view of the martyr, it may be about achieving a higher level of fulfillment or reward, not about the loss of a role. On the other hand, accepting martyrdom because if you didn't you would no longer be considered part of the group is one example of avoiding the sadness of loss of group identity, the loss of which is deemed greater than the sadness of loss of life.

2.10: GUILT IN CONNECTION WITH COMBAT

As veterans have told me about their feelings of guilt, they have often described situations that even they acknowledge were impossible to be remedied, no matter what they did. They sometimes feel guilty that they survived and someone else died miles away, with no possible connection to their behavior. In order for us to blame ourselves for such a loss, we must have it in us somewhere — though not in any logical knowledge system — that part of preserving our identity includes preserving belief in our having supernatural powers.

This belief may be ingrained from childhood, when adults invariably hold a child responsible for behavior beyond the child's level of maturity ("I know you can color in the lines better than that little Johnny"). Similarly, in military training, recruits are held to impossible standards of performance. I have often heard veterans refer to themselves as "playing God" when they were in combat. Of course, if they were gods they were very weak ones, with only the power to destroy (and only then with risk to themselves), no ability to escape, and without other godly powers such as creation.

So, rather than accepting the loss of an identity that includes belief in one's supernatural ability, and accepting the fear or sadness caused by this loss (partially due to rejection by a parent or military organization), people have self-anger (guilt) as a form of punishment. The illusion is maintained that the super-ability is still possible, and that the people or organizations claiming it is possible are right. So, guilt is the punishment that maintains a person's identity, as well as of the authority of the agency that makes the rules.

The alternative to guilt is the acceptance that you never could be the child/soldier that you were expected to be, and that the person/organization that had those expectations is not the perfect entity that you thought it was. The sadness or fear that goes with this kind of loss can be worse than guilt, as horrible as that is.

This choice to accept supposedly the worst feelings possible — those that go with being in Hell, instead of the feelings that go with loss of identity — is interestingly represented in Milton's epic poem *Paradise Lost*. In it, Satan discusses the possibility of repenting and returning to Heaven. He then dismisses the idea with the statement that it would be "Better to reign in Hell than serve in Heaven." (p. 144) May we suppose that for Satan, serving in Heaven means that there would be grief in giving up his kingship role, and fear of being subservient to God, and that he would rather accept the feelings one has in Hell than confront these other emotions?

In addition to the sadness and fear that go with the loss of identity, there is another cost to giving up self-blame and guilt. That loss is of a romantic view of the world and people, one in which one can achieve an identity, such as the true soldier or the true artist. It is a state in which no real work is necessary for righteousness, one that contradicts the idea that all people are always in jeopardy of failure. Acceptance of never having been able to be perfect counters the view that character is everything, and calls for acceptance of the view that we are defined by our current actions.

In this new non-perfection view, one has to accept the painful feelings that would go with the loss of this self-image. We also have to dedicate ourselves to doing the work necessary to prevent us from giving in to temptations. This work would include acknowledging the power that outside forces have and will always have on us — that we cannot just make ourselves perfect once and for all, that we have to work at covering the same ground every day. This is the essence of 12-step programs derived from Alcoholics Anonymous and the "one day at a time" approach. The relevance of the 12-step analysis is increased if we consider anger something that one can be addicted to.

Our choice becomes to accept the sadness that goes with acknowledgment of our imperfection, and the fear that goes with knowing that we will always have to work hard to avoid the pain of failure and loss, or accept the guilt that keeps coming as we persistently fail to live up to the idealized image we hang on to.

The above analysis should not be taken as a general condemnation of guilt. Like anger, it has real value, including survival value. In many situations, especially in the military, expectation of the ability to do the impossible is essential to training and performance. Among the eventual negative consequences is vulnerability to self-anger (guilt) in the case of failure. The habit of unreasonable expectations takes over where it does not belong, and destructive guilt and anger become "solutions" to the problem of accepting sadness that the impossible self-expectations cannot be met.

So how can we have the reasonable and unreasonable expectations both be true? The only way I know how to do this is to have two kinds of truth, one for life-and-death situations and one for everyday life. In the world of combat, motivational concepts such as "We leave no one behind" and "Death before dishonor" use guilt as a means to an end. In the everyday world, however, common sense must prevail (e.g. "Taking turns is good," "Let's talk about it").

2.11: FEELING AND EMOTION

Describing sadness as an emotion and pain as a feeling brings up the question of the difference between a feeling and an emotion. The word "emotion" is impossible to define to everyone's satisfaction; however, the definition offered here is generally consistent with what is found in scientific writings on the subject.

We will consider emotion to be a state of being or a neuropsychological pattern, such as sadness, fear, anger, or happiness — that is, a reaction to one's relationship with other people, the world, or life. Facial expressions, physiological reactions, and body sensations are usually associated with different emotions. Emotion can be in awareness or out of awareness. When an emotion such as fear is in awareness, it is still an emotion, but it is also a feeling.

Feelings such as hunger, thirst, or physical pain also involve a body sensation, or a perceived body sensation, but unlike emotions, they don't occur because of a person's relationship with other people, the world, or life.[2] As the chart below shows, feelings are things we know we have, and some (e.g. hunger, pain) can never become emotions. When they are hidden, emotions are not feelings, but can become feelings when they are known

---

2   The neurologist Antonio Damasio (1999, 2003) has written extensively about the relationship between emotion and feeling. As far as I can tell, my writings generally agree with his more detailed and extensive expression.

or felt. When anger hides fear, the anger is a feeling and emotion; the fear, though, is only an emotion.

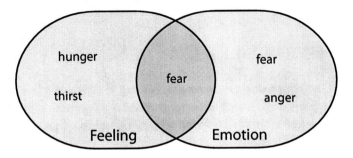

Figure 3

Emotions can be mixed. Someone can be both happy and sad about the same event, and want to block both emotions. Happiness or affection can trigger anger resulting from fear of the loss of someone — the more you care about them, the more the loss would hurt. This is probably why some combat veterans have trouble showing, or even feeling, positive emotions when returning home. These emotions exist, but are hidden.

2.12: SURPRISE

I am not against all anger, or even violence. This is about the anger you don't want to have, the anger you later regret.[3]

---

3 I included this here, in this way, because it sometimes needs to be repeated to break through some peoples' certainty that those who are helping to control unwanted anger are against all anger.

2.13: BACKGROUND FOR MENTAL HEALTH PROFESSIONALS: THOUGHT LEADING TO EMOTION

The definition of emotion above implies that there must be some kind of thought that goes with emotion. If this is so, then emotion, unlike body sensation or thought, would appear to not be a pure state, distinct from thought, because it relies on thought to help determine it. Though there has been much debate about this among psychologists, the prevailing view is that we can have emotion without thought (Zajonc, 1984). To illustrate: We could stimulate part of the brain and get a person to show the physical and biological signs of fear without putting that person in a scary situation that would produce fear thoughts. However, as life is actually lived, this pure state of emotion is very rare, as there are not many people running around with electric brain probes to stimulate pure emotion.

We may also consider that for emotions such as fear to arise there must be some preliminary idea of a threat. We could call this a thought. But there is a difference between, for instance, thinking that a car is driving toward you and thinking that the person behind the wheel is out to get you. There is also the memory of fear, which can come without the thought that one is under attack. In the example of Pavlov's dogs, who were given an electric shock when a bell sounded, and later showed fear when the bell was sounded without the shock, they probably didn't consciously think of the connection between the two. Rather, the fear reaction automatically occurred, bypassing thought. There will be more about this later in a discussion of the memory of emotion (see Chapter 3.6).

Pure thought without emotion might be one way to describe a computer's output when it solves a problem. However, in people, even the simplest thought is usually connected to some kind of feeling.

When discussing this idea of pure emotion with my clients I sometimes invoke the *Star Trek* character Mr. Spock. According to the *Trek* story, the residents of Spock's home planet Vulcan attempted to banish emotion after nearly destroying themselves with anger and war.

Spock, a half-human, half-Vulcan, defines himself as completely rational and without emotion. Though he is able to justify everything he does rationally, it is an open secret, and running joke, among the characters that his emotion exists, but is hidden. When I compare Spock with the talking computer on the bridge of the starship *Enterprise*, my clients can easily see the difference between hidden emotion and nonexistent emotion, and how impossible it is to have emotion completely absent from the decision-making process of a human, or even a Vulcan.

2.14: EMOTIONS: FEELINGS VS. THOUGHTS

Before we get to more specific examples it is important to mention a problem that many people (including therapists) face in identifying emotions: the confusion between emotions and thoughts (beliefs, ideas).

Emotions and feelings are internal experiences for which each person is the final arbiter of truth — "the decider." Thoughts are more easily accepted as open to discussion and modification. When emotions and thoughts are mislabeled for each other, a problem can arise. If a thought is labeled a feeling, then it is more easily considered out of bounds for reconsideration, which can lead to people getting stuck in thoughts that may not be very true or useful. This is especially problematic if the thought is tied to destructive anger.

For example, an employee may say he feels betrayed by his company, or a veteran by his country.[4] In true emotion terms he feels anger, and as time goes on, he may become increasingly estranged from others as his anger does not lessen. It may be perfectly true that the person was betrayed; however, by calling it a feeling, two possible sources of relief from this alienating "feeling" are blocked:[5]

1. If the betrayal could be viewed as a thought, then its validity and limitations could be explored in discussion, and it might be modified to lead to less destructive anger. For example, he might see how it wasn't everyone who betrayed him, or how some of what he saw as betrayal might have been the simple incompetence that no one is completely immune from.

2. If anger could be identified as a feeling, the formula for looking under anger for blocked sadness or fear might lead to at least partial resolution of the anger,

---

4   It cannot be reasonably doubted that this country, and other countries, have at times betrayed their veterans. On this subject I recommend the book The Wages of War by Richard Severo and Lewis Milford. But betrayal has not been all there is to the relationship. Despite its failings, veterans still overwhelmingly love their country, and are more likely to help it, than they were a few years ago.

In my discussions with veterans I have sometimes suggested the following. When we are young, our country is like our parents: It is powerful, and we reasonably expect it to look out for us and reward us for our fidelity. At some point, however, the relationship must change. Our parents get old and need our care, which we very often can provide. Similarly, our relationship with our country must also change when we become adults. Our country is still overwhelmingly powerful, but it needs to become like our child — we must try to lead it, to take responsibility to try to help it grow to its potential. Because of its size and strength we cannot dominate it. We have to encourage it and be active with it, but, like a big old Baby Huey when it rolls over, we have to be careful not to get crushed.

5   Some of my colleagues have argued that betrayal is a feeling/emotion as well as an event. As we casually speak to each other, that is usually OK. However, when feelings and emotions have led people to profound problems, then a more precise analysis of the word "betrayal" is necessary.

and an eventual move to solve the problem that led to the betrayal. This may help others to not be betrayed in the future. However, I am afraid when it comes to war, some betrayal is an inevitable part of what makes it Hell.

One way to sometimes determine if a word represents a thought or a feeling/emotion is to consider if the word describes the cause of the experience. For example, "abandoned" would be a thought because it describes the cause. "Fear" or "sadness," on the other hand, are emotions because they do not describe the cause.

I cannot leave this section without mentioning that this confusion of thought with feeling/emotion is not necessarily all bad. It can put us in touch with important information that cannot yet be verbalized. Sometimes our intuition is correct and saves us. The problem is that too often, calling a thought a feeling/emotion is the end of the process, and leads us to block discovering necessary information.

CHAPTER III:
THE PREVENTION OF DESTRUCTIVE ANGER

3.1: HOW DOES THIS KNOWLEDGE HELP PREVENT DESTRUCTIVE ANGER?

If the job of anger is to prevent feeling fear (among other emotions and feelings), then logically, acknowledging and tolerating fear would take away anger's job and keep it from appearing. As it turns out, sometimes this fear does not have to be fully felt; sometimes identifying a fear by name is enough to prevent anger.

Even naming a fear, though, can potentially bring up all manner of painful experiences. In explaining this we will discuss the memory of emotion. In the example of Sam and Joe (Chapter 2.5) we considered how anger can block current fears of losing a job, or the loss of esteem, or sadness at the loss of a friend. In the following example, we will discuss those current emotions brought up by a road rage situation, as well as the role of memory of emotion.

3.2: ROAD RAGE AND ANGER PREVENTION

Road rage is a problem so prevalent that there was speculation a few years ago that it would become a psychiatric diagnosis. (OK, it was probably a publicity stunt, but the idea did get mentioned, and it is a big problem.)

A road rage situation is often created when someone cuts us off or drives dangerously. If we must respond quickly, we probably have immediate surprise and fear, which we may or may not feel. The next reaction is the feeling of rage. When I discuss this with clients who have problems with road rage, they usually acknowledge the validity of the following analysis: The anger is sometimes followed by aggressive acts against the offending driver, which perpetuate, or increase, the danger of the situation.

If we were to use Venn diagrams to visualize emotion and feeling in this situation (as we did in Chapter 2.11), it would look like figure 4, below.

In figure 4 the activating event of being cut off in traffic (A) wakes up fear, which in this case is fear of a crash. The fear then moves toward awareness, where it can become a feeling (the central area).

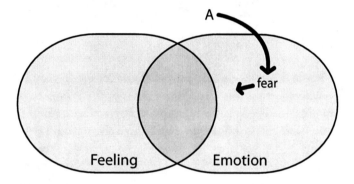

Figure 4

In figure 5, below, emotion is being blocked at the right-hand barrier between emotions and feelings. For the person in this example, that wall is thick. We could call this thickening a high level of emotional numbness or callousness. (This blocking is not usually bad. If we didn't have some of it, we would all be walking

around like babies, showing emotion at the slightest provoca-
tion.)

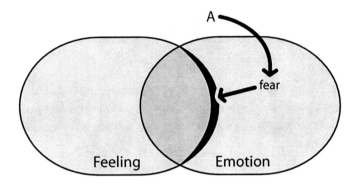

Figure 5

In figure 6, we see the addition of the anger mechanism (which
we will refer to as the "anger machine," because it can keep creat-
ing anger as needed).[6] It responds to the activation of fear and
makes sure the fear does not get through the wall and become a
feeling. If the fear does get through, the anger machine tries to
push it back down.

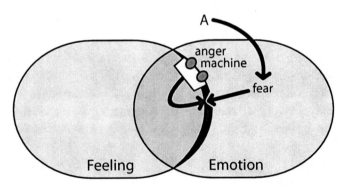

Figure 6

---

6   We can view all emotions as being produced by a machine. If this
book's focus was the problem of excessive fear, it would explore the
nature of the fear-production mechanism. We might even discuss how
fear can block anger (which it does sometimes). However, in those
cases, the anger itself is blocking an emotion as well, which can even be
fear. Fear can occur without having to block something else.

In the central area, feelings and emotions overlap. In the space on the left are feelings (such as hunger or tiredness) that can never become emotions. Similarly, on the right side are emotions that can never become feelings unless they cross into the center. When fear is felt, it is both a feeling and an emotion; when it's hidden and not felt, it is only an emotion.

3.3: SO, WHY THE ATTACK?

Since the new aggressive act increases risk, it is clear that the goal must have moved from protection against danger to something different. The new goal is one that was mentioned in the example of Sam and Joe: blocking emotion that would come with the loss of respect, or self-esteem, from being treated as if you are powerless.

Now we can add a new factor: the memory of emotion. This doesn't feel like a memory; it feels like the emotion itself. In this case, it is the memory of fear. Let's say the person being cut off is a combat veteran who has had the experience of being ambushed, which in some ways is not so unlike being cut off in traffic. Iraq war veterans, for instance, may have experienced an ambush on a highway very much like a U.S. highway. So they must fight off their fear in the current situation as well as their memory of the ambush, in which their fear may have reached the level of terror (sometimes this is called a flashback). Here, the high amount of fear may lead to the need for sudden and extreme anger to hold it down.

The memory of fear not only relates to combat; it can also relate to being disrespected, perhaps resulting from childhood bullying, and maybe also being berated by a parent for having been bullied. (The memory of emotion will be discussed in more detail in Chapter 3.6.)

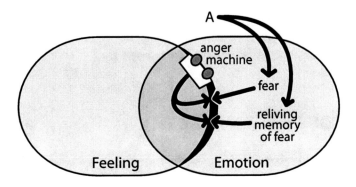

Figure 7

Figure 7 shows the event A waking up both current fear and the reliving memory. Later, there will be another diagram showing more of the relationship between current emotions and the memory of emotions.

3.4: THE HEART SOLUTION TO ROAD RAGE

As you get into your car, say these words to yourself:

I'm entering a potentially dangerous situation, with people driving big metal objects at high speeds. If something unexpected happens, it will be scary, and I might get very angry. If I do get angry, it will be to hide the fear I have. I might worry about more than my safety, but also about whether I am respected. So anger might spring up to block my fear that the seemingly inconsiderate driver doesn't respect me.

What you say to yourself may be further modified by your personal history, such as a reminder that you are no longer in the situation that contains the memory of fear.

When you start using this exercise, do it every 10 minutes while driving. After a while, you will probably be able to do it less often, and eventually only remind yourself at the start by saying "fear."

OK, I know nobody is really going to say that all to himself, but you get the idea. Consider at least trying it. Practice is essential.

Earlier, I suggested that you look for situations in which anger might block other emotions, then practice naming those emotions. Now I'm suggesting that you do an exercise every 10 minutes while you drive. Where do you draw the line? When is it enough?

To answer this, I ask you to consider your life. What do you do every day, or frequently, to maintain something important? Do you brush your teeth? Do you floss? Do you do physical exercise, or practice a sport? How do you decide what is important enough to practice? I don't know what your answer will be, but when you make a decision about practicing the skill suggested here, please consider it, and further exercises, in that context.

In exploring the above questions, I once gave a questionnaire to 14 people to whom I was teaching the HEArt ideas in a stress management program. Only two said they practiced the stress relief or mental health exercises daily. This was particularly troublesome since they were all getting help, at considerable inconvenience to themselves, for problems with stress. The good news was that 13 out of 14 said that they brushed their teeth every day. So if you try giving these stress exercises the same level of importance as tooth-brushing, it might help.

3.5: AN OBJECTION TO THE ABOVE

One objection I have heard to the suggestion that road rage and chasing down an offending driver are dangerous behaviors: "If I don't go after the person who cut me off, how will he ever learn to drive better? I have to go after him to save others." When I hear this I think to myself, *Give me a break*. But I respectfully remind the person, "It is my job to help decrease anger when that is desired, so if you think your road rage is helping public safety, then I can only hope I am not nearby when you are driving in education mode."

I might also ask if the client has ever cut someone off by accident, and if being attacked by the person they cut off would be a sensible way to help them become a better driver. The absurdity of an attack on an offending driver is magnified by the fact that almost everyone acknowledges that they have cut others off by accident. When someone does it to them, they know there is a good chance it is an accident and is not worthy of an attacking — and possibly fatal — response.

There is another side to this objection: Perhaps the aggression is motivated by the need for an orderly world,[7] one in which wrongdoing is punished. Some clients have eagerly latched on to this explanation when it is discussed. The fear that the world will deteriorate unless vengeance is extracted appears nobler than the desire to preserve one's self-image. However, engaging in retribution that may injure innocent parties and leads to excessive penalties for a common driving mistake makes this "orderly world" hypothesis appear weak, even to themselves, when they think about it.

3.6: THE MEMORY OF FEAR AND THE INTENSIFICATION OF ANGER

To fully understand the concept of fear re-emerging from the past, we need to discuss how memory works. The mind can be divided up many different ways, but one of the most important involves two types of memory. They have been thought of as short-term and long-term memory, though recently, they've been referred to as reliving and historical memory. If something is in reliving memory, being reminded of it causes you to feel like it is happening again.

---

7   This may be related to the experimental findings of Kahneman (et. al. 1986) in which subjects make choices to enforce fairness as some cost to themselves. Janoff-Bulman's (1992) often-cited work about trauma may also be considered here. If the principal burden of a traumatic experience is, as she says, the destruction of deeply held beliefs that the world is meaningful and benevolent, and that we have worth, then our acting to undo that loss might be expected.

An extreme example is seen in a full "flashback." The stereotypical example, which does actually happen at times, is of a combat veteran being surprised by a loud noise, like a car backfiring, and reacting by heading toward the ground, feeling fear and looking for an attack. In this case, the loud noise woke up a memory of being in battle that was stuck in reliving memory (technically, part of what is called non-declarative memory). It is the nature of most, but not all memories, to move into historical memory. After combat events have moved to this memory system, when the veteran hears the loud sudden noise, he or she may have some startle response, but instead of looking for a follow-up attack, the person might say to himself, *That is the kind of noise I heard in combat. I know I'm not there now.*

Another simple non-combat example might also help clarify. Let's say a person was in a car accident. It was a bad accident — scary, with lots of damage, but minor physical injuries. Two weeks later the person is watching TV and sees a similar accident. That person starts to feel fear again. Does it make sense? Almost everyone I ask says yes, which is true if the memory is still in the reliving memory system. However, if the memory has mostly moved over to the historical system, then the person might feel lots of other things: relief in not being hurt, compassion for the person on TV, worry about paying the insurance deductable, etc. However, the person would not feel the reliving type of fear.

Why doesn't the memory move over like it is supposed to? A likely answer is that movement mostly happens during sleep, while a person is having "reliving" dreams/nightmares, or what could be called sleep flashbacks. The amount of emotion during the dream wakes the person up, so the work is stopped. The movement might also happen while a person is awake, but when he or she tries to get away from the memory, the work is stopped. Waking flashbacks are the same way: The memory comes up, but the connecting mechanisms are blocked. It might be that some kinds of chemical blocking of a person's emotion level will allow for the natural processing of memory to take place. The psychiatric medications currently available can block emotionality, but from my perspective, not in a way that promotes this transfer of memory. It's possible, though, that new treatments will be able to accomplish this.

There is one more complicating point that should be mentioned. In some special cases, anger can also be found in reliving memory, having come up to block fear in the past. In this case, that anger can also add directly to the current anger.

Therapy and time can be helpful in resolving the problem of having reliving memory add to fear and then increase the anger response. The more events that are moved to historical memory, the less extra fear there is to deal with.

3.7: GENERAL BACKGROUND: FIELD AND OBSERVER MEMORY

There is a distinction between two kinds of visual memory that I have only seen discussed in research, but may help us better understand changes in memory (Robinson & Swanson, 1993). "Field" memory involves recalled visual impressions, as if an event is being relived. In field memory you can't fully see yourself in the picture — you can't see your back, or face or head, only what was in front of your eyes. The other type is "observer" memory, in which the scene can be seen from any perspective — above you, below you, from behind you. When people are asked about their visual images of past events, the memories tend to move from a field to an observer perspective. They can also move back and forth. Clearly any event that is remembered from an observer perspective must have been at least partially processed; the mind must have done something other than just recording it. When you get an observer memory, much of the memory is memory that something happened, not of it happening.

3.8: PHANTOM LIMB PAIN

One more example might help here. There is a not-uncommon phenomenon called "phantom" pain (Sherman, 1996),

A THEORETICAL DESCRIPTION OF BRAIN/MIND
PROCESSING OF POTENTIALLY TRAUMATIC EVENTS

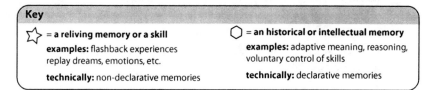

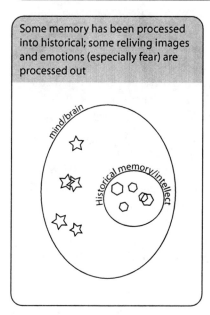

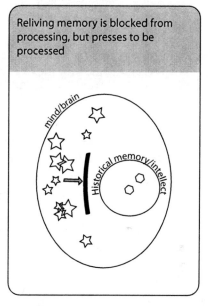

For reliving memory to be processed into historical memory during waking it has to be allowed to come to, or near, awareness, and the events it involves can then find a path to adaptive meaning. When this happens, unnecessary or maladaptive emotional responses, such as fear when the event is over, are processed out. Necessary or adaptive emotions and skills are not processed out.

Figure 8

experienced by people who have lost a limb. Sometimes they feel that their arm or leg is still there and feel a great deal of real pain, including sensations like cramping and burning. Researchers have eliminated the possibility that the pain is coming from the nerve ends in what remains of the limb. Since the limb is gone, the only remaining possibility is that somehow the pain is being first experienced in the brain. This could be an example of a memory being experienced as pain, a kind of flashback as found in post-traumatic stress disorder. This pain is often not alleviated by medication.

Added evidence that it is experienced as the memory of pain comes from some studies of the treatment of phantom pain with a kind of psychotherapy called EMDR (Eye Movement Desensitization and Reprocessing; see Appendix 4). This method is typically used for the treatment of post-traumatic stress disorder. To explain it in simplified form, the client is asked to bring to awareness a traumatic memory (one considered to be held mostly in reliving memory), then follow the therapist's hand with his eyes as the therapist moves it back and forth. While this does sound odd, the method is quite well-accepted by scientific organizations that evaluate methods of psychotherapy. EMDR does appear to change the way traumatic memories are held; it seems that they become more like historical memories than reliving ones. There are now several case reports in which phantom pain was alleviated with this method of therapy (Schneider, 2008).

3.9: PSYCHOTHERAPY AND THE MOVEMENT OF MEMORY

Since we don't have any medications proven to chemically promote reliving memory to move to historical memory, we have to rely on other ways to try to accomplish this. For most traumatic memories that are stuck in reliving memory, a natural processing occurs over time. Most people can easily see this if they remember an emotionally painful event from early in life that was devastating at the time, but now is not a problem, or even seems funny. Sometimes, despite the pain, one is grateful because of the important lesson learned.

The other way this happens is through psychotherapy. Psychotherapy is an odd business. Much of what is now called psychotherapy has been part of healing rituals since the beginning of human culture (Frank & Frank, 1993). If we consider psychotherapy a kind of learning, recent scientific discussion suggests two general forms in which this could take place. One is when new learning overlays old learning — kind of like new habits taking the place of old. The old is still in there, just not active, though it could become active again (e.g. going to an AA meeting instead of drinking). If we consider therapy in terms of memory instead of habits, the reliving memory does not immediately move into historical memory — rather, it is just blocked out more effectively. When something occurs that would have awakened the reliving memory, it also wakes up another intellectual memory, or a new habit that blocks out the old.

The other form is when new learning modifies the old, so the old is no longer the same. This is called reconsolidation. If the old habit occurs again — that is, the old way of thinking, feeling and acting — it is not because it has been activated, but because it has been relearned. In reconsolidation, the old memories move over to the historical/intellectual memory system, and become different.

This is not necessarily an either/or situation. Different methods of psychotherapy likely emphasize one of the two processes. In my experience, EMDR is more likely to lead to a reconsolidation effect than the other popular scientifically supported methods, such as cognitive therapy or imaginal exposure. Even when the therapy just blocks the memory more effectively, it still can foster eventual reconsolidation.

3.10: ON NAMING EMOTION

Going back to the road rage example, if the goal is to prevent anger from occuring, or to keep it at a low level, the most important step in accomplishing this is to begin the process before the anger situation (being cut off in traffic) occurs. After recognizing that anger arises to block fear (naming fear, the HEArt Level IV skill), we can then employ the Level III skill to figure out what the fear was about. Once the fear is named, the anger becomes irrelevant — it doesn't have a job — and our task is to understand what the fear is about and what to do about it.

Once we are already in a situation where dangerous anger is starting, or has already occurred, then we must use whatever will work: getting away, or relaxation, or thinking our way out of it. In my experience, the more you practice the Level IV skill, outside of real situations, the less anger will arise to have to be controlled. With enough practice, anger can almost always lead to us asking a question like "What am I worried about?"

3.11: A MORE COMPLEX EXAMPLE

Let's examine an example of destructive anger in a parent waiting for a child who is out late. The parent gets more and more angry until, when the child finally returns, the parent is enraged and, perhaps, abusive. Perhaps the parent justifies the harsh treatment as a way of trying to keep the child from repeating the dangerous behavior of staying out late. However, the parent may regret the intensity of the punishment after recognizing that it is counterproductive. If the anger and the angry behavior are acknowledged to be mistakes, then what could have motivated them?

Let me propose that it was fear for the child, fear for what might have happened. For a combat veteran, the fear and anger may be heightened by the reminder of what it meant when comrades did not return from patrol when expected. If the parent can acknowledge the fear — ideally by saying it — and attend to the message of the fear, then the parent's actions will more likely be protective of the child and the child's future.

How would this look inside the parent's head? Here are two of many possibilities.

Non-HEArt:

Little Johnny is late with the car; something might have happened to him. Maybe he crashed. He was probably speeding. I bet he got to goofing around with his friends, that little jerk. When I get my hands on him...

HEArt:

Little Johnny is late with the car; something might have happened to him. Maybe he crashed. He was probably speeding. I bet he got to goofing around with his friends, that... wait a second, I'm getting angry. What am I worried about? I'm worried about his getting hurt. Maybe I'm reminded of something from the past. Remember, this is not then. Maybe I should call his friends' parents.

(Notice that some anger is there to block the fear, but it was caught quickly and the worry is able to do its job, of figuring out what the danger was and how to deal with it.)

One objection I have heard is that it's sometimes necessary to punish bad behavior, and the HEArt approach lets people get away with anything. I disagree. HEArt is about the emotion, not the behavior; planning effective punishment requires rational thinking and a cool head. Angry punishment is often regretted and apologized for, and mostly teaches people to hide from you. This behavior is more likely to be abusive and perceived as meaning that the parent doesn't care or wants to drive the child away, physically and/or emotionally. Well-thought-out punishment — because the parent accepts the worry and shows it in a way the child can see it — comes from love and is more likely to make sense and to be stuck with.

Perhaps now is the time to answer a couple questions some might be asking: No, I am not a veteran. Yes, I have raised teenagers.

3.12: AFTER ACKNOWLEDGING THE EMOTION

In both cases above, identifying the underlying emotion led to more productive thinking and behavior. In one example the road rage is prevented; in the other the child will be greeted by a concerned and loving (but still, perhaps, irritated parent). However, sometimes, even just naming the painful emotion can bring up a flood of feeling. Perhaps the child coming home late wakes up traumatic memories stuck in reliving memory.

First, do not look for painful emotions when it is not safe to do so. In the examples above, the painful emotions are looked for before the anger situation occurs, or at least before contact with the person who would receive the anger. After the anger situation begins, it may be safer to use the early-level HEArt skills, such as calming oneself or thinking rationally. It is also a good idea to look for the hidden emotions after the anger situation in order to deal with lingering seething.

This brings us back to the question of what to do with the pain of emotions when it is not hidden. How is one to manage this without getting angry again or using drugs, alcohol or another self-destructive distracting behavior? Because naming the emotions[8] can lead to them being experienced, there must be a way to make it so they do not become intolerably destructive. This is how Levels I, II and III integrate with Level IV.

This will be discussed in greater depth in Chapter 5, but briefly, this is the time to use the mindfulness exercises of Level II to tolerate the emotion until it subsides. Our rational, philosophical and spiritual insights can help. These can sometimes be directly accessed because they are related to the more essential emotions of fear and sadness. For fear-based emotions, the fear is used as a signal to figure out how real the threat is, and how to protect yourself. For sadness, knowing the loss that the sadness is about helps clarify what was not lost. There are also situations in which humor, which combines Level II and Level III solutions (see Chapter 5.6), may be invoked.

---

8 This means simply saying the word, for example: "I have fear" or "I have sadness." This isn't as easy as it sounds. It sometimes takes an amazing amount of time for some people to say the word "fear," even when they seem to want to say it. There is much more about this in chapter 4.

3.13: EMOTIONS AND THEIR ENERGY

Emotions have a kind of energy path to them. When they are identified and expressed, they seem to tire,[9] allowing a person to more fully consider the situation. This is particularly true for sadness. When one fully experiences the sadness connected with a loss, and the sadness tires, one can remember what hasn't been lost: the value of the relationship that did exist, and the permanence of that.[10]

As I've presented the HEArt program to clients, I have asked hundreds of them if they have noticed this "tiring of sadness" at gatherings after funerals. People are sad and the sadness is acknowledged and accepted. Then, at some point, people begin to talk about their good memories involving the deceased, and even laugh. This is an example of how when the emotion is accepted, it seems sadness expends its energy. After the loss is acknowledged, we get to remember what we have not lost and feel better. This does not mean that the sadness will not return, only that our memory of who we have lost does not have to dominate us and our lives. The memory can inspire us.

Clients have sometimes told me that this doesn't work for them — they feel the sadness, but it doesn't tire. It is true that grief, even when not blocked out, often comes back. But in my experience it is not so destructive, and the positive aspects do come through more. On the other hand, some clients for whom sadness does not diminish, even though they feel it, acknowledge that rather than seeing the sadness through to its end, they start to get angry and call themselves names for having had the sadness and tears. When the sadness is blocked before it runs its course, it is more difficult to get to what we have not lost.

---

9   That isn't exactly how it works, but it seems that way. What probably happens is that the opposing forces in the nervous system, the sympathetic and parasympathetic, bring us back toward a state where new emotions can occur.

10   In his novel The Portrait of a Lady, Henry James creates a scene in which Isabel attends her cousin Ralph as he is dying. Ralph says, "I'm very tired. You said just now that pain's not the deepest thing. No — no. But it's very deep. If I could stay ... It passes, after all; it's passing now. But love remains." (p. 623)

For those with the biological illness of depression, this natural balancing may not work, and they may need psychotherapy or even medication directed at depression. On the other hand, sadness is not all there is to depression; sometimes there is anger, especially at the self.

3.14: THE BUILDUP OF ANGER VS. THE ANGER MACHINE

Anger, like other emotions, has a path of energy. People often feel calmer when it is expressed and sometimes think doing so is the best way to get rid of destructive anger. They think anger accumulates, like in a big tub, and that if they just keep emptying the tub, they will eventually not have that anger anymore. But what really happens is that the anger keeps coming back.

I think this is because anger is more of a skill for getting rid of things in the short run, and a habit, than an accumulation of emotion. The emotions accumulated are fear and sadness (remember the reliving memory discussion), as new frightening situations and losses occur and are not processed. Those emotions are what keep coming back. If the person becomes angry as a blocking mechanism, those stored emotions are still in the bucket waiting to have something wake them up again.

When angry behavior gets people feeling better in the short term, I think what happens is this: People have sadness or fear, they experience a kind of helplessness over loss, and when they get angry, they are reminded that they are not completely helpless and that they do have some power. A person might sometimes be so desperate to be reminded of his power that even that momentary feeling is enough to make even some pretty bad consequences of anger seem worth it. I don't doubt that there are a few people sitting in prison who still believe that it was worth what they did in anger.

Here is a situation that arises with some of my clients who are veterans. As Memorial Day approaches, the ads for Memorial Day sales are everywhere. He or she might think something like:

All that death, all that pain, and what does it mean? I can get half off on a mattress in a Memorial Day blowout sale. I'd like to show them a real 'blowout.'

That was the nice version. The veteran then stays home seething, instead of going to a family picnic and appreciating the things he or she does have. Who can argue that the veteran doesn't have a right to be angry?

Let's say our vet does not want to be so angry, even if there is a perfect right. By going directly to Level III skills and rethinking the situation, one might say, "OK, they weren't there, so they don't understand. They are just ignorant. I used to be ignorant about war myself, so I'll just ignore that ignorance and go about my day. Maybe someday, some advertising director will have a kid in the war, and it won't seem so cool to have a Memorial Day blowout."[11]

Although this solution relies on thinking to realize that no immediate angry action is necessary, it does not use the underlying emotions to find what might be a more satisfactory end to the undesired anger.

Going through those emotions helps find what the anger is blocking. The obvious answer is sadness, which is part of what a memorial is about. It is proposed here that being aware of that sadness and grief, and paying personal respect to those being memorialized, gives those emotions a logical focus and allows some peace to be found through spiritual or philosophical beliefs.

This is not to say that the Level III thinking above, perhaps leading to some social action, would not also be possible. Finding the sadness attached to the loss of meaning of Memorial Day might help one get there.

---

11 A little anger still may come out. But there are other spiritual and philosophical possibilities with no anger attached. Perhaps someday a veteran, not out of anger, will prompt a veterans' organization to put a commercial on TV discussing the commercialization of the holiday.

Another benefit of the emotion-first over the thinking-first approach is that even if you can't think of a logical way out of the anger immediately, you know that it is about some kind of pain. That knowledge can help you to not blow up and keep looking for useful answers. Finally, going through the anger to identify what has been lost may lead to action to try to regain it. Perhaps someday a veteran, not out of anger, will do something like prompt a veterans' organization to put a commercial on TV discussing the commercialization of the holiday.

3.15: A SONG

In the song "Raindrops," by Dee Clark, the singer portrays a man who has lost his love and finds "raindrops" falling from his eyes. He sings:

> *There must be a cloud in my head*
> *Rain keeps falling from my eyes*
> *Oh no, it can't be teardrops*
> *For a man ain't supposed to cry*

Let's leave this chapter with a question: Will the singer of this song resort to anger when he realizes that it is unlikely that the water on his face is rain?

CHAPTER IV:
PARTICIPATION

4.1: INFORMED CONSENT

It is time now to present more ideas to practice, based on the suggestion that once an underlying/hidden emotion is identified, and actually named[12] (it does help to actually say it out loud, or at least write it), the anger no longer has a job and might cease to come up. Be warned again, though, that sometimes identifying the underlying fear or sadness can be more painful than expected and difficult to tolerate. This can result in even more anger, especially if we bail out and don't keep examining the underlying emotions and the causes of them (see Chapter 3.12). Let's ease into our work with these powerful emotions by first considering anger in another person. If you find yourself applying these ideas to your past and the emotion becoming truly overwhelming, please use the Level I and II skills and consider contacting a licensed counselor.

4.2: EXERCISE 1: DESTRUCTIVE ANGER YOU HAVE OBSERVED IN OTHERS

Think of a situation in which you have seen someone display destructive anger that he or she, no doubt, later regretted. See if you can speculate as to what emotions were being hidden by the anger. A clue will be to figure out what he or she was in danger of losing, or thought might already be lost just before the anger. Use the Sam story (Chapter 2.5) as a hint. Write the name(s) of the hidden emotion(s).

---

12   Research by Matthew Lieberman and his colleagues (2011) gives experimental support to the idea that naming emotions has an effect on how they are experienced.

4.3: A REMINDER ABOUT KINDS OF MEMORY AND EMOTION

Before we go on to the next exercise, it is important to remember that the past can bring extra intensity to anger or rage. Remember, each person's history contains experiences that influence how anger is expressed. It is not just what happened, but where the experience is held in memory. When something resides in reliving memory and is awakened, it feels like the event is happening again.

If we go back to Sam, let's say sometime in his past Sam was betrayed by a friend and still hasn't fully gotten over it. (It is partly stuck in reliving memory.) Then not only will Sam face the fear and/or sadness of the current situation, he might also face the emergence of emotions of which he might not be aware.

This can be seen in its most extreme form with severe trauma. Let's say the betrayal Sam faced was in a life-and-death situation, like combat, in which there were feelings of terror or panic (or just emotions of terror and panic, blocked by numbness). When he gets in a similar situation, the memory may naturally reawaken, and if the memory is in the "reliving" system, he may have some of the same feelings. If the memory is in the historical/intellectual system, he may be reminded of the original situation, but instead of experiencing similar feelings, he may be reminded of the lesson he learned: that he survived that betrayal, so he can survive this one.

When people talk about "flashbacks," they are referring to (even if they don't know it) the experience of having a memory in the reliving system reawakened. The reawakening can be partial — just the feeling, like in the example above — or just visual, or it can be complete, where people temporarily think they are fully reliving a past event.

4.4: OBSERVING DESTRUCTIVE ANGER IN YOURSELF

Perhaps you want to take the risk of naming your own hidden emotions. Since our anger is there to protect us against even more painful feelings, it is important to be careful when and how we address these. I recommend that you start by focusing on future issues, and not try to take on what might be very painful past events. If you have very painful traumatic past events, contact a licensed therapist — particularly one versed in EMDR — to help with the processing of these memories and emotions.

As our focus moves from the anger of others to the destructive anger in ourselves, I suggest you consider a possible future situation in which you might find yourself destructively angry. Then consider what underlying emotion might be blocked by the anger.

As you do this you may feel more comfortable, and not even feel the named emotions from the fear or sadness family. Or you may feel worse in some ways: The phrase "sadder but wiser" may apply. If you feel increased anger, it is probably because in this exercise you have discovered something new that bothers you about the situation, and the anger is coming up to block that new bad feeling.

If that is the case, then it is time to look again at that painful feeling and understand what it comes from, and what it has to teach.

We have many choices in life, but not always the choice to be happy about something. Some people have found that their spiritual or philosophical beliefs, when they can be invoked, can help with even the most painful situations, and even find ways to reconnect to what is good in the world.

4.5: EXERCISE 2: YOUR FUTURE DESTRUCTIVE ANGER

Imagine a time in the future when you may get angry, more angry than you want to. The situation could be having to wait at a doctor's appointment, or seeing a family member, or practically anything else. Give the situation a name and rate the level of anger you think you might have, or have currently, from 0 (no anger) to 10 (the highest it could be).

Name of situation:

Number rating:

0   1   2   3   4   5   6   7   8   9   10

See if you can figure out what the underlying sadness or fear/ worry will be. A clue will be to figure out what you might be in danger of losing. Use the Sam story as a hint.

Write the name of the emotion(s) being hidden by anger. See appendix 1 for some hints. The answer will probably be in the fear or sadness family. It should not be something in the anger family, like frustration or irritation, as these are not hidden:

Having figured out what the underlying emotion could be, see if you can use this knowledge to guide a productive response. Consider Sam again (Chapter 2.5). He is worried about losing his job, but what is the actual likelihood of that happening? What can he do to keep it? (Note that focusing on anger will not help him figure this out.)

Let's say the loss is something that cannot be prevented. How do you manage the fear or the sadness? Do you know that if you do not fight with the fear or sadness (when it is safe to feel them) that they tend to lessen, even if they do sometimes come back? What spiritual or philosophical ideas or resources do you have to deal with those things that can't be changed?

Examine your feelings about the situation now. Rate your anger again from 0 to 10:

0   1   2   3   4   5   6   7   8   9   10

Write down[13] the names of any other emotions you know you have about the situation now, and rate them on the 0-10 scale. Rate the level of the emotion before the exercise and then after it.

Emotion name:

Before:

0   1   2   3   4   5   6   7   8   9   10

Now:

0   1   2   3   4   5   6   7   8   9   10

Emotion Name:

---

13   All this writing and rating may seem like a pain, and I under-stand that asking people to do this may risk turning them away from the project. However, it is just this kind of attention to the work that makes it have the best effect. To not offer it would be to not offer the best suggestions in psychology.

Before:

0   1   2   3   4   5   6   7   8   9   10

Now:

0   1   2   3   4   5   6   7   8   9   10

By this time you may be feeling better about the anger-causing situation. On the other hand, as said above, you may feel worse in some ways. If you feel increased anger, it is probably because in this exercise you have discovered something new that bothers you about the situation, and the anger is coming up to block that new bad feeling. If that is the case, then it is time to look again at that painful feeling and understand what it comes from, and what it has to teach.

4.6: EXERCISE 3: DAILY PRACTICE TO REDUCE ANGER

In this exercise the goal is to set up a system to predict, on a daily basis, what might occur to keep anger from arising at all. You might be wrong in this prediction, but daily practice can help make this search for the underlying emotion a more automatic skill. Some people object to this exercise, asking why they should seek out troublesome emotions every day. Maybe they are feeling good at the time they scheduled practice; why bum themselves out? My response is that if you are reading this book for yourself, then you have already tried that, and it hasn't worked. But if you think the strategy of not preparing for anger will start to succeed anytime now, what can I say?

On a daily basis, and ideally at a set time, consider the following:

1. What might happen today that would get you destructively angry?
2. What emotion might be hidden by the anger?

3. Write the name of the hidden emotion in the box provided.

For example, you might walk by a TV, hear a story about a war, and get angry or enraged. The hidden emotions might be worry about the troops, or perhaps sadness over things you are reminded of. (Remember: Don't write what you feel; write what emotion would be hidden by anger. It is always tempting to think a psychologist is asking you to write what you feel. I am not. I am asking you to write what you don't feel, what is hidden.)

Week	M	T	W	Th	F	S	Su
4/12	Worry sad						

Figure 9

If you practice naming hidden emotions on a daily basis, remember that acknowledging these emotions might immediately reduce your anger. But you may still have to confront the power of the emotions you find. It is then that you must use your wisdom (see Appendix 5) to recognize that:

• What is feared may not be so dangerous.
• If it is dangerous, how to protect against it.
• If protection against it is not possible, how to accept it in the least destructive way.

I have noticed that participants in the HEArt presentations sometimes do not follow through with practices, even if they find the ideas valuable. Some have been more willing to try when offered the following as the first-day practice square:

Figure 10

4.7: ACCEPTANCE

The previous mention of "acceptance" sounds something like the Serenity Prayer, written by the American philosopher and cleric Reinhold Niebuhr (see Sifton, 2003) and often discussed in Alcoholics Anonymous. A popular form is:

> *God, grant me the serenity to accept the things I cannot change, courage to change the things I can, and the wisdom to know the difference.*

As I have discussed this with my clients it has been clear that some do not have a solid sense of what they mean by the word "accept." I think acceptance has several parts, all of which are not easy to do. Some of the parts listed below will have different meanings, depending on whether they are about accepting what we have done or accepting what has happened to us. However, all aspects are in some way relevant to both.

Week	Monday	Tuesday	Wednesday	Thursday	Friday	Saturday	Sunday

HEArt Log

Figure 11

1. **A clear understanding of what event actually occurred**. This does not mean judging it, but instead, knowing the facts. If you accidentally hit a person with your car, what happened is that you drove your car and hit someone, which is different than saying what happened was that you ruined someone's life, or an accident happened. The latter two might be true, but that doesn't provide enough clarity about the events themselves.

2. **A clear understanding of what led up to the event**. What were the factors that contributed? Were you speeding? Did the person cross the street against the light? Were you intoxicated?

3. **Acknowledge, and perhaps feel, the emotions that go along with the event, and their meaning.** If there was loss, know the sadness of as many aspects of loss as you can understand. These may include loss of — as was shown in Chapter 2.9 — people, things, or even parts of yourself.

4. **Learn from the event.** If there is knowledge to be gained about yourself, others, or life, find it.

5. **Act on what you have learned.** This may include fixing what you can fix, or the Serenity Prayer's[14] "change what you can." In the Serenity Prayer, this comes before accepting. But as outlined here, accepting can lead to re-seeing what you can change.

6. **Find your spiritual or philosophical beliefs that will make any necessary pain less destructive.**

   Acceptance and punishment. I did not give this part of the definition a number, and saved it for last because thinking about these concepts is beyond difficult. I think a lot of people might say true acceptance can't happen unless a person suffers the appropriate punishment. However, I have not, and never expect

---

14   For more on the Serenity Prayer, see in Appendix 5.

to say to someone else, "Stand up and be punished for everything you think you have done wrong."[15]

Part of the problem in addressing this issue here is that it involves philosophy as much as it does psychology — that is, the finding of meaning. It is not about the law, and can't pretend to be so. So if we are talking about accepting what the law says, I would say leave that to the lawyers.

Ideas about punishment are considered more fully later in Appendix 3, On Forgiveness, especially in the section on self-forgiveness.

I hope the above exercises have been helpful, and can be helpful for you in the future. Even if you do decide to keep using anger to block more immediately painful emotions, at least you may be more aware that there is a choice.

4.8: RETURNING TO IDEAS FROM LEVELS I, II, AND III

After you understand and practice using the advanced skills in Level IV of the HEArt program, there is reason to hope anger will not arise as often or as destructively. It will be prevented earlier. But it may still be a problem, partly because anger can come up so quickly that we don't have the chance to think about the underlying issues and emotions. That is when the information featured in the first three levels and further elaborated on in the next chapter might be most helpful. It is my experience that most people have considered many of the general ideas in the next chapter. But some details of those ideas may have not been considered, and might be very helpful.

---

15   Polonius: "I will use them according to their desert."
Hamlet: "God's bodkin, man, much better! Use every man after his desert, and who shall 'scape whipping?"
— Hamlet, Act II, Sc. 2

CHAPTER V:
LEVELS I, II, AND III

5.1: LEVEL I (PHYSICAL PRESENCE)

As said in the introduction (Chapter 1.1), sometimes it is best to walk or even run away. Some people who are particularly concerned about the effects of their anger manage their lives so there is little contact with others. They especially avoid crowded non-structured activities or places, such as shopping malls. I have heard vets refer to "bunkering in," meaning staying in a place they set up to be safe, often a basement.

Sometimes mental health professionals make a pitch for people to get out and about. I can't give any general advice on this subject, because I can't know how dangerous it actually is for a particular person to get out. This book is intended to help you fully understand the desire to stay away from others, and what to do about it if you decide to engage the world in a generally peaceful manner.

5.2: LEVEL II (PHYSIOLOGICAL CONTROL)

Here we can add a couple of calming exercises. These Level II skills may be helpful in breaking the cycle of thoughts and feelings that can increase anger. To review that cycle:

- Event occurs, fear begins to rise >
- Anger is triggered >
- Thoughts that increase anger become solidified >
- Feeling of anger increases >
- Thoughts of being under attack increase >
- Anger feeling increases, etc.

The more you practice calming exercises, the more likely you will be able to use the skill of calming anger-related body reactions when you need to. It may help also if you attach a word or name to the exercise, such as "peaceful" or "calm," so that that word will become attached to the feeling state.

These are called "calming" exercises instead of "relaxation" on purpose. For some people, relaxation is seen as a dangerous state, in which you are particularly vulnerable. However, everyone recognizes that sometimes, being too jumpy or excited can increase the danger of a situation. In such cases, calming is recognized as a safety measure. That is what is intended here.

5.3: CALMING EXERCISES

Presented here are three of many possible breathing exercises I have found helpful for myself and clients. You can easily find many others in books on stress management and on meditation. Not everyone will like all of them, so experiment.

Exercise 1:

- Take a deep breath and exhale slowly through your mouth.
- Repeat.

Exercise 2 (Alternate nostril breathing):

- Close the right nostril with your knuckle.
- Inhale deeply.
- Switch and close the left nostril (yes, opening the right one).
- Exhale completely.
- Inhale deeply.
- Switch and close the right nostril.
- Exhale completely.
- Repeat.

Exercise 3 (Counting breaths to four and starting over):

- Inhale deeply.
- After you exhale, count "one" silently.
- Inhale deeply.
- After you exhale, count "two" silently.
- Inhale deeply.
- After you exhale, count "three" silently.
- Inhale deeply.
- After you exhale, count "four" silently.
- Repeat for five minutes or so, or longer if you like.

If you lose track, start counting again with one. There are several versions of this exercise, based on what your mind does when it is not counting. You can let it just wander, you can focus on a problem, or you can focus on a pleasant fantasy.

Exercise 4 (Combination of breathing and mental imagery):

Practice letting the mind construct or remember a place in which you believe you are maximally safe and feel as calm and relaxed as possible. Imagine yourself there — imagine what you would see, what you would feel in your body, what you would hear. Do that for a while.

Like any other skill, if you want to have the skill of calming yourself, you have to practice it. The more you practice it, the more likely you'll be able to call it up when you need it. Good luck.

5.4: LEVEL III (THINKING RATIONALLY)

For almost all other mental health works on problem anger, the Level III skills are the essence of the message. Philosophers such as Seneca, the Roman statesman, have also taught these ideas for millennia. More recently, in about 1600, Shakespeare wrote in *Hamlet*:

> *...there is nothing either good or bad but thinking makes it so... Oh God! I could be bounded in a nutshell and count myself a king of infinite space... (Act II, Sc. 2)*

The message is that we rely more on what we *think* of things than anything else. We all know there is some truth to this (even if sometimes we don't know it when we need to). If someone touches us and we *think* it is a gesture of dominance, we have one reaction; if we *think* it is a show of desired familiarity and affection, we have another. The HEArt program values the insight of what has come to be called the "cognitive therapy" position. However, as the preceding pages attempt to make clear, the best way to get to the insights of reason is often through recognizing the emotions that are tied to our reactions, and are often hidden.

In using rational thinking to prevent or manage destructive anger, I recommend the work of the late Albert Ellis who I think is the best proponent of modern mental health thinking in the area. There are also other very good teachers on how to employ rational thinking for good social functioning with whom most mental health professionals are familiar.

As suggested in Chapter 1.1, I think there are two basic, related questions to consider with destructive anger:

1. Will the anger-based behavior be worth the cost?
2. Is the anger based on a reasonable assessment of the situation?

The first question is particularly useful in stopping an anger-behavior reaction quickly. Like the Level I skill, it is a primitive, emergency method for stopping a regretted behavior response. The second, a fuller, rational consideration of the situation, often needs to wait until the threat has passed. It is here that HEArt and rational consideration work best together. If one applies HEArt and recognizes the underlying emotions, then there is a sound basis for rationality to provide useful further analysis.

This can easily be seen in the example of Sam (Chapter 2.5). Once the roots of his anger — the fear of losing his job, or sadness about the loss of his relationship — are acknowledged, then rational consideration about the real risks can take place. Maybe Sam will fully consider how the supervisor will hear Joe's story and realize that it is not true. Maybe Sam will understand the stresses he was reacting to, or the almost infinite other number of possibilities. Perhaps this can best be simplified by asking ourselves two questions about the other person's actions:

1.   What were that person's motives?
2.   What am I worried about?

The HEArt program is based on the idea that the second question will more quickly prevent or circumvent anger, making the first question easier to answer.

To return to the Level II skills, Albert Ellis' (1996) well-known formula for beginning to use reason to overcome distress, published in many books, unfolds as follows:

A — an activating event, which then produces

B_1 — irrational beliefs, which lead to

Cs — consequences (problem behaviors or emotions)

Ellis' model, Rational Emotive Behavior Therapy (REBT), has people consider rational beliefs (B_2) to produce more adaptive behaviors and emotions. The HEArt program suggests that if the Cs are anger, then recognition of the painful emotions behind the anger makes the B_2s easier to find.

To return to Shakespeare, the passage that begins with "Nothing is good or bad, but thinking makes it so" starts by bowing to the importance of what we think, but ends with the phrase "were it not that I have bad dreams." Shakespeare is acknowledging that reason will get us far, but will not solve all the mysteries or pain. What causes the bad dreams — what Shakespeare does not address — is emotion that is stuck in memory, which sometimes has to be addressed through something other than logic (see Chapter 3.6 and Appendix 4).

5.5: SPIRITUALITY AND REASON

While spirituality and religious belief are ultimately based on faith, which is different than reason, they still belong in Level III. This is because our angry behavior often does not make sense, given the spiritual beliefs we proclaim. If we believe we are in fact our "brother's keeper," and we would do unto others as we would have them do unto us, then much of our anger and angry behavior do not make sense. Appendix 3 takes a close look at forgiveness and discusses these issues in detail. If you look at that section, you may be surprised to see that forgiveness is not always recommended and that anger — though not destructive anger — is respected.

5.6: HUMOR

Humor has a funny role in this business of levels. I think it is both a Level II and Level III skill, and it has probably caused as much anger as it has prevented. It changes emotion directly, as calming or meditation exercises do, but it also contains alternative ways of thinking about something — ways that may not lead to anger.

Humor can be a way of accepting sadness that goes with loss, so as to not be overwhelmed by it. When Abraham Lincoln responded to a critic, "If I were two-faced, would I be wearing this one?", he was not feeling the full weight of the pain of his lack of classical beauty, which may have hindered him in life. Yet he was not denying the pain either. Humor had the effect of reminding him that he had the power to rise above what many thought were his aesthetic limitations, but without resorting to destructive behavior that would later be regretted.

In another example, the following cartoon draws attention to the limitations of words which might, as the phrase goes, "push your buttons," while invoking a feeling of mirth as the viewer contemplates the artist's attempt to draw a teddy bear.

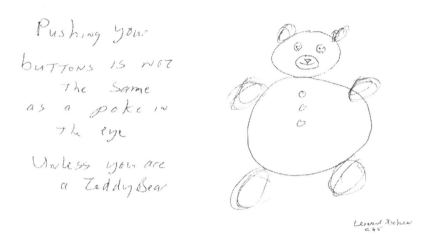

Pushing your
buttons is not
the same
as a poke in
the eye
Unless you are
a Teddy Bear

Figure 12

5.7: GENERAL BACKGROUND: REASON, HEROES, AND VILLAINS

As we attempt to employ reason to understand situations, we employ a basic understanding, or philosophy, of the world and humanity. The two contrasting positions are Romantic and what I will call here Contextual. The Romantic position holds that what we do reflects our basic nature, which is good or bad. We are either a hero or a villain. It is an all-or-nothing position. The Romantic position emphasizes labels. So if someone transgresses (activating event) and their trangression is taken as a sign of their character (evil), then we are almost obligated to be rightously angry.[16] From the Romantic position, anger and attack would seem to be rational.

The Contextual position holds that our behavior is more determined by our situations, and what we have learned, than our nature or character. This position holds that labels or names are

---

16 "Nothing is more uplifting in life than rightous anger."
— Philip Roth, "American Pastoral"

not usually appropriate for people, who can change. So if we call a person a coward, it suggests that that person is now and will always be a coward, like a chair is always a chair. We all know this can't be completely true of people, because each of us can find an example when we gave into our fear and another example when we did not.

I will argue here that the Contextual philosophy usually makes more sense, and that if you start with that idea when you consider life's problems, you can figure out how best to change things that need to be changed. The pure Romantic position leads to the least possibility of change and the most emphasis on punishment and causing pain to stop the people with supposedly bad character. (Please see Appendix 3, On Forgiveness).

This is not to say that the Romantic position is always wrong. Sometimes in combat, or in other struggles, we must call on every ounce of our emotional and/or physical strength to succeed or even survive. In these cases, using the part of us that labels, that calls us "hero" or "coward" — perhaps in the voice of a drill instructor, coach, parent, or even playmate — may save us and the people who rely on us. Sometimes, people must be severely punished for acts so they won't be repeated, even if we know they are not fully evil. Nobody can, or should, live in one or the other of these philosophies all the time. I have never seen or heard of it even being possible. The trick is living in the one that makes sense at the moment.

CHAPTER VI:
THE EXPRESSION OF EMOTION TO OTHERS

6.1: THE DEVELOPMENT OF EXPRESSION OF EMOTION IDEAS

Earlier in this book, I compared the four levels of the HEArt program to attaining a college degree in the prevention of destructive anger: associate's, bachelor's, master's, and Ph.D. (In Appendix 9, I discuss them using a martial arts perspective.) When I give presentations on this program, I tell audience members that they received their GED for showing up. However, similar to college, even after one has attained the highest degree in HEArt, more learning can still be done — a post-doctoral degree, so to speak. The post-doc of HEArt is expression of emotion to others.

When I began working with these ideas about anger and other emotions with groups of clients, the emphasis was on telling others how you feel. It was an effort to help people communicate and cooperate by getting the focus on how others affect us, rather than on casting blame. The popular formula, which I have seen attributed to Haim Ginott (Goleman, 1995), goes "When you say _____, I feel _____."

As you can see, this section about communicating with others does not appear until after a lot of discussion about emotion inside the person. I had several reasons for focusing first on knowing our own emotions:

1. Clients were having a very difficult time identifying emotion. For one thing, they couldn't distinguish emotions from beliefs.

2. Important pain hidden by my clients' anger wasn't related to anybody they could talk to and improve their relationship with.

3. Even if we tell others what we feel, it might not improve things between us, so the only benefit we might be sure of is self-understanding.

Below are the potential benefits of sharing the emotion with others. They are both internal and related to the relationship:

1. When we share an emotion with someone else, and don't just name it for ourselves, it promotes taking extra care to be clear and accurate.

2. When others find out that you have emotions, it helps them see you differently, as a person, not as a stranger or an adversary.

3. There may be an enhanced connection with the other person as he or she sees that you trust them with your emotions.

4. Numbers 2 and 3 may allow the other person to hear that your point of view is not just about emotion, but about doing things differently.

As with most things, there is another side. Here are some potential risks of sharing emotions:

1. The other person may take advantage of you because you now appear to be weak. This person might make fun of you, smirk and call you a baby, and tell everyone else what a weenie you are. Then you will have to be outrageous to prove this person is wrong and prevent further emotional damage.

2. You may be accused of being a manipulative jerk who is pretending to be sensitive to trap the other person and get your way.

3. You may open up some painful feelings in yourself, which will be difficult to deal with.

That was a rather strong presentation of the negatives — I don't want to be accused of stacking the deck in favor of sharing emotions. Though there are risks of doing so, this does not mean one should never take the chance. Even if you think the other person may respond negatively, if you don't think that it will cause too much pain or rage to kick in, then it might still be worth the chance. (A little later on, there will be some examples of various outcomes of sharing emotions.)

There is an additional potential benefit of the negative response, if you can take it: It can give a better understanding of what is going on with the other person. It may be that the other person is truly not interested in anything but gaining advantage over you. Or the other person may be so scared from his own past, or your past together, that he has to block your efforts in order to protect himself. I have had several clients tell me they received a negative reaction from a family member after sharing their emotions, seemingly because of the family member's underlying fear. In these situations, I recommend patience, as well as family therapy, which may have an increased potential of being helpful, as the emotions are now better understood.

6.2: SOME GENERAL POINTS ABOUT COMMUNICATION STYLE

Communication can be seen as occurring in two forms. One conveys facts (content) and the other informs about the relationship. The second, sometimes called meta-communication, shows itself through body language, tone of voice, vocabulary choice, etc. So if you tell me your name, your name is the content communication, and if you shout it in my face with a menacing look, to intentionally (or unintentionally) communicate to me that you should not be messed with, that is the meta-communication. When using HEArt with someone, we try to pick which words we use, our tone of voice, etc. It is important that we invite the impression that we are equals in the discussion and that the communication is not made from weakness. This may seem impossible when the communication is about fear or sadness, but it is not.

Consider the example we see on TV all the time: A mob boss says to his intended victim, with exaggerated sincerity, something like "You hurt my feelings when you show me this disrespect." Obviously, this statement of painful emotions is not necessarily a sign of weakness. The goal in HEArt is to find the position between subservience and dominance. This can be difficult, but less difficult if, when you say you are hurt, your goal is to truly say what you feel, not to prove anything to yourself or someone else about your worth as a person.

Back to the mob boss for a minute. Though he may not seem serious when he says he is hurt, the fact is, he does have negative emotion. He is unhappy that he is not respected, and worried that if people can get away with defying him, he will lose his power and that, in his violent world, he could be killed. His fear is more important than the anger or the indifference, which he shows by ordering the killing of the "disrespecting" victim. After all, why would he bother being violent if he wasn't worried?

If your answer is that he is perverse, and likes hurting others for its own sake, then I ask that we consider how he got that way. There may be a biological predisposition. Much has been written about this, and I will not attempt to review the whole field; however, also to be considered is research by Lonnie Athens, which is interestingly summarized in the book "Why They Kill," by the award-winning science writer Richard Rhodes. Athens explores the histories of convicted murderers and concludes that they went through stages of development to get to murder. The first stage, which he calls Brutalization, includes "violent subjugation, personal horrification, and violent coaching." (Rhodes, p. 112)

A second offering is a poem of uncertain origin:

> *I and the public know,*
> *What all school children learn,*
> *Those to whom evil is done,*
> *Do evil in return.*

6.3: HOW TO NAME YOUR EMOTION TO ANOTHER PERSON

Here is a formula for rehearsing the statement of emotions to others according to HEArt principles:

1. Be clear in your own mind that your primary goal is to identify and state an emotion.
2. Identify the emotion(s), other than anger, for yourself.
3. Politely ask if the other person is available to listen for a few moments.
4. Honestly
5. name
6. emotion(s)
7. about a behavior or situation
8. so that others can or will want to hear.

Then:

9. Listen for, and to, the response.
10. After the response, if necessary, remind the person that your intention was mainly for them to know what you felt. If possible, thank them for listening.

Here is the formula with notes written to facilitate practice:

1. Be clear in your own mind that your primary goal is to identify and state an emotion.

If the primary purpose of the exercise is to manipulate the other person into doing something different, then the value of the next step (identification of the emotion) may be lost because the search for an underlying emotion might not be honest. (See section 5.1 about benefits and risks.)

2. Identify the emotion(s) for yourself.

As stated in the previous sections, anger is very unlikely be the primary emotion — even though it is real, it is not the essential core. You can think of anger as a house built to stand on a foundation of sadness and/or fear. The house is real, but cannot be built without a foundation, and if the foundation collapses, so does the house.

3. Politely ask if the other person is available to listen for a few moments.

This step has considerable value in making it clear that there is at least minimal respect for the other person's rights. It also helps remind us that lots of people generally walk around preoccupied (thinking of something important or just kind of spaced out). Just starting in on a discussion without letting the other person prepare will lead to a defensive response. We all know that this is true for ourselves, but sometimes forget it with others. Philo of Alexandria, in the years before people started having last names, is reported to have said something like "Be kind, for everyone you meet is fighting a great battle." We don't know at which moment the battle might be at its worst. So, if you ask if the other person is available to listen and he or she is not ready, you can try to figure out a better time. If a time can't be found, then you have sufficient warning that this may not be a good person with whom to share emotions.

4. Honestly

If your communication isn't honest, it isn't going to effectively prevent or reduce your own anger. Also, consider that "honest" means true and relevant. You may have all kinds of thoughts or feelings about the other person that are better left unsaid, because they are not relevant to the issue at hand. Consider the earlier example of the kid who is late getting home. You may believe that this child is stupid, and be sad about that, but that opinion and sadness are irrelevant to helping the kid do better.

    5.   name

Say it or write it, but state it. The actual statement of the word seems to matter. Giving your full attention to the word is what is essential for getting the most value out of understanding your emotion. You may have to speak of your anger, but if so, be sure to make clear the importance of what other emotions it is based on (see examples of this in Chapter 6.4).

    6.   emotion(s)

See Chapter 2.14 on thought vs. emotion.

    7.   about a behavior or situation

See #8, the next item.

    8.   so that others can or will want to hear.

That means no name-calling, and no burying the emotion word in a lot of arguments for your point of view. In fact, people often use any expression of a thought or idea or an argument to distract from the emotion, and you must be careful not to fall into this temptation yourself. This is where the chief communication about the relationship takes place. It is the main place where you show that the communication is something shared between equals.

This is a good opportunity to introduce one of the most valuable ideas in psychology, brought to us by the social psychologists. That is "the fundamental error of attribution," which social psychologists Ross and Nisbett (1991) define as "people's inflated belief in the importance of personality traits and dispositions, together with their failure to recognize the importance of situational factors in affecting behavior." (p. 4)

Avoiding character analysis in your description will help keep you from making a mistake in describing how the situation got the way it did. It has more to do with the history of events than character.[17]

    9.   Listen for, and to, the response.

Almost everyone needs to be reminded of this sometimes — even psychologists, even me. Occasionally, when confronted with something particularly difficult, I want to jump in and respond quickly. I find it helpful to say to myself, *Listen, listen.*

    10. After the response, if necessary, remind the person that your intention was mainly for them to know what you felt. If possible, thank them for listening.

What you say to the other person is sometimes essential to remind yourself what you are trying to do. It is really easy for people to forget that the most important thing is to know one's own emotions. At some point, after the emotions are clarified, you can get on with talking about changes that can be made.

If you think about stating your emotions to someone else based on the arguments made here, I strongly recommend you first practice the skill by role-playing with someone with whom you feel very comfortable. Psychotherapists are usually very good at this.

6.4: SOME SAMPLE DIALOGUES

Here is a simple situation — it's simple because it is not about an ongoing relationship, which has emotion attached to it:

You go to the doctor's office, where the receptionist gruffly tells you to take a seat. You feel angry immediately. You seethe, but

---

17 I recently heard a story about a man who survived a rare, serious illness that resulted in days in a coma and more than 200 days of hospitalization. When he listed the reasons he survived, No. 1 was that he was a tough SOB. No aspect of the medical care he received was on the list.

you know you can control your behavior. You step away (Level I skill).

Next, you use Level IV skills to explore what emotion(s) the anger is blocking. The candidates are, as ever, from the fear and sadness families. (Remember you don't yet feel them — they are hidden — but you can figure out they do exist.)

To find the hidden emotion(s), ask what was or may be lost in this situation. Some possibilities are:

- Self image (for letting someone talk to you this way)
- Confidence in the medical staff (if this lack of competence extends to their medical practice)
- Your health (which you may have already been worried about, making an angry reaction more likely)
- The peaceful mood you had attained before going to the doctor
- The reawakening of past losses

Looking even at this brief list, we might see causes of underlying sadness or fear. According to the underlying theory of HEArt, simple recognition of sadness or fear can reduce the level of anger, helping you take the best action to satisfy your major goals. However, if you want to make the situation clearer for yourself, as well as for the person whose behavior initiated the emotion — and maybe improve their behavior and your mood — then, when you have enough emotional control to speak to the emotion, you might say to the receptionist:

You: May I tell you something?

Receptionist: OK.

You: I am worried about the care I will get here. The way you told me to "take a seat" left me concerned about my care.

Receptionist: I'm sorry.

You: Thank you. (You walk away, or ask about how long the wait will be, etc.)

It's relatively[18] easy to like using HEArt when it produces this kind of result from the other person, but remember, the main idea is to identify the emotion to yourself. The response from the other person, if it pleases you, is just gravy. To better illustrate this, consider the following alternative reaction. As you read this, remember that what is being suggested is not easy, and you are the only one who can decide if it is worth the cost:

> You: *I am worried about the care I will get here. The way you told me to "take a seat" left me concerned about my care.*
>
> Receptionist: *We are very busy here. Take a seat.*
>
> You: *OK, thanks for listening.* (After you use your Level I, II, III and IV skills, you can plan how you will contact the person's supervisor.)

This is a very different result, and if you think that it will lead to destructive behavior, don't even try it. Instead, consider using HEArt internally: Walk away and identify the other emotions under your anger. This does not mean you have to "take it." There are other effective, nondestructive ways to be assertive, such as complaining about your treatment.[19]

HEArt is about identifying and making peace with the emotions which, when not addressed, lead to destructive anger. So in this situation, the anger returns when you are again dismissed. The situation now is even worse, because you have made yourself

---

18   I say "relatively" because it is difficult for some people to get past labeling themselves weak for this type of response. It takes some getting used to.

19   This has been a frequent topic of discussion with my clients, who often say it doesn't matter if you complain to a higher- up, because nobody does anything about it. I then ask them how they like it at their jobs when somebody goes over their heads to complain. How many complaints does a boss put up with? When they are supervisors, how do they treat employees who are complained about? These questions usually end most of the objection. But, I might anyway throw in the idea that one reason people think complaining doesn't matter is that it makes it easier to not bother complaining. And, again, this complaint is not HEArt; it is another kind of assertiveness. It is asserting your belief.

vulnerable to this person, who has responded with disrespect. The potential loss of face is enormous, as are the accompanying fear and sadness.

The most basic problem is understanding the fear and sadness, which produce the anger. If the anger comes from blocking fear or sadness that would cause you to lose your self-image or dignity, then the solution must come from understanding that your most important dignity does not come from how others treat you, but from how you think of yourself. If you have fear based on the idea that if you let this person get away with treating you this way, then you will always be the victim, then it is important to examine if this is a legitimate fear. If it is, then it is important to consider what is the most effective way to prevent the outcome without being destructive to yourself physically, emotionally, spiritually or in any other way.

In this situation, I think the best emotional solution is compassion. It is a pathetic thing for the person who can do no better with the demands of his or her job than to be curt or rude (perhaps to block underlying emotions?). When you do successfully find your compassion, you may still have concerns about your care from the doctor, but you do not have the self-image-related pains. You have the right to be angry, but you may be better off not exercising it. This is sometimes called enlightenment.

As the examples unfold below, you will see that using HEArt with another person is not always the way to improve your relationship. The way the other person reacts to your statement of emotion may lead you to want to end, or diminish, the importance of that relationship. Or, as shown below, it may put the other person off. These are all reasons why it is important to go into the encounter with the primary goals of clarifying your emotions to yourself and having the "satisfaction" of knowing you told the other person what you felt. Improvement of the relationship should be considered a fortunate secondary outcome, while worsening of relations could be an unwanted, though perhaps instructive, side effect. If the main goal is to improve relations, then the activity should not be considered HEArt, though it may still be a very respectable form of assertiveness (this will be further discussed in Chapter 6.5).

MORE COMPLEX EXAMPLES OF ONGOING RELATIONSHIPS:

You don't like the way your significant other has told you to take care of some household chores. You know they need to be done, but you still don't like the way you were talked to. You have let your significant other know how you feel about it a million times, and are ready to give up on getting her/him to change.[20] You decide to use HEArt — *What the hell, might as well give it a try*, you think. You can't help but hope this will change how she/he talks, but you decide it is more important to know and be clear to her/him what your emotion is. You feel anger, but then consider what emotion might be underneath it: something in the sadness family or something in the fear family?

If it is sadness, it is about what was lost; if it is fear, it is about what you might lose or might have lost. You consider what, if anything, has been lost. If you think you have lost respect, or that it might be going that way, then the emotion is in the fear family. You approach your significant other:

> You: *I'd like to tell you something, if you have a minute to listen.*
>
> Other: *OK.*
>
> You: *When you talk to me the way you just did, I get angry, but underneath that is worry, worry about respect in our relationship. That's it — I just wanted to tell you about my worry.*
>
> Other: ......

The other person could respond to your use of HEArt in an infinite number of ways. Here are a few possibilities, followed with your possible responses, most of which continue to use HEArt:

---

20 This seems like an appropriate place to mention, that, if the your overriding goal is to improve one's your marriage, I recommend the work of John M. Gottman, even if he does occasionally call thoughts feelings.

Other: *Wow! That is the first time you ever told me what you felt. Thank you.*

You: *I'm glad you feel that way.*

Other: *I just can't hear that now.*

You: *OK, but thanks for letting me tell you that much.*

Other: *What are you up to? What devilment are you getting into?*

You: *I know it is different than how I usually am, but it is what I feel.*

Other: *Don't try that on me.*

You: *Thanks for listening.* (Maybe walk away and get some distance so you don't blow up, then think about what you want to do next.)

Other: *Now there is something we can talk about.*

You: *OK, let's talk.* (At this point, you may use something other than HEArt to talk about your relationship.)

Other: *I'm sorry.*

You: (Prepare for this possibility based on your goals, even if you think it is unlikely.)

Other: *If you want respect, you have to show respect, and you are the least respect-showing jerk I have ever met.*

You: *OK, but I still wanted you to know what I felt, and it is worry.*

Other: *Like I said, if you want respect, you've got to show respect.*

You: *Maybe we should see a counselor to see if we can work this out.*

6.5: STATING EMOTIONS TO OTHERS VS. STATING DESIRES TO OTHERS

In standard psychology teaching about getting your thoughts across, there is an emphasis on many of the same things discussed here, such as consideration of the other person's situation, clarity of thought, and avoidance of appearing that you want to dominate. These efforts are usually about getting across the idea that you want some change in behavior from the other person.

I have gone back and forth for a long time with the question of including a request for behavior change, of trying to get the other person to do something different as part of HEArt. I have finally decided to exclude it from the basic formula. Asking the other person to change as part of the formula may be a very good way to achieve that goal. However, when the request becomes explicit, it can distract too much from the primary goals of making peace within yourself and telling the other person about your emotion. A discussion about changing the other person's behavior must take into account everyone's needs and desires, and goes much easier when emotions — about fear, especially — are clearly stated.

6.6: I CAN'T GET HEART TO WORK FOR SOME PEOPLE

After years of working with HEArt, I have learned that not everyone will find all the HEArt suggestions worthwhile. These people are in good company: The great Roman philosopher Seneca might agree with them. He might say that the Level III lessons, working with thoughts, are the highest form of education in this matter. Seneca and others have written that painful emotions and anger could be fully mastered and eliminated by reason. They didn't have much regard for identifying hidden emotions, and have not even necessarily agreed about their influence.

However, I think Seneca would agree with my suggestion about talking to others by putting your case in a way that the other person could and would want to hear. My clients who don't agree with the way emotion is discussed in the HEArt program have still expressed appreciation of the part that helps them be more aware of their anger and express themselves with greater consideration. I am pleased that they found something helpful in this.

APPENDIX 1:
LIST OF EMOTIONS

Psychologists have differing opinions about many aspects of emotion. Though they divide up basic emotions in various ways, this list compiles families of emotions, as well as the main actions associated with each emotion.[21]

Remember, emotions occur without us knowing whether we have them or not. However, we know when we have feelings.

FEAR FAMILY (ASSOCIATED ACTIVITY: TO ESCAPE, HIDE)

Terror

Panic

Dread

Fear

Worry

Edginess

Uneasiness

Embarrassment

Trepidation (a little curiosity?)

Shame

Humiliation

---

21 Prepared with assistance from Drs. Julia Smith and Brandi (Booth) Burque.

SADNESS FAMILY (ASSOCIATED ACTIVITY: TO SHUT DOWN OR WITHDRAW)

Grief

Despair

Anguish

Sadness

Regret

Discontent

Loneliness

Unhappiness

Wistfulness

Hurt

Melancholy

Dejection

Disappointment

Dismay

Distraught

EMOTIONS ASSOCIATED WITH CONCERN ABOUT OTHERS (SOME WITH A WORRY COMPONENT)

Pity

Compassion

ANGER FAMILY (ASSOCIATED ACTIVITY: TO ATTACK)

Rage

Hatred

Anger

Irritation

Guilt (anger at self)

Jealousy

Scorn

Disgust

Resentment

Wrath

Frustration

Hatred

Aggravation

Grumpiness

Spite

Loathing

Fury

HAPPINESS FAMILY (ASSOCIATED ACTIVITY: TO APPROACH OR TO TAKE IN)

Love

Happiness

Joy

Contentment

Pride

Curiosity (an approach emotion, but may have neutral feeling)

Hope

Gratitude

Wonder

Amazement

THOUGHTS/BELIEFS OR BEHAVIOR SOMETIMES MISTAKEN FOR EMOTIONS

Betrayed

Threatened

Appreciated

Insulted

Rejected

Manipulated

Defeated

APPENDIX 2:
EMOTIONS AND THE BODY

The experience of emotion is rooted in the body, and therefore, physical sensations are related to an individual's current emotional state. Developing an awareness of what is happening in your body is very important in understanding your emotional experience.

There are common physical sensations and reactions that go with emotions and feelings. Some are unique to a specific emotion and some overlap. As C.S. Lewis wrote in *A Grief Observed* (1961), "No one ever told me that grief felt so like fear. I am not afraid, but the sensation is like being afraid." (p. 19)

Facial expressions can sometimes, but not always, also be tied to emotion.

What may you be aware of?

- Tension in the stomach, sometimes referred to as "butterflies"
- Lump in the throat
- Muscle tension
- Increase or decrease in breathing rate
- Increase or decrease in heart rate
- Perspiration rate
- Change in posture
- Change in the tone of your voice
- Change in your ability to maintain eye contact
- Change in pupil size (more noticeable in others)

APPENDIX 3:
THINKING AND FEELING ABOUT FORGIVENESS

The ideas about forgiveness discussed here have been around a long time. What is proposed is one possible combination of philosophy, the science of psychology, and what the author has learned from interactions with combat veterans, other clients, and personal experience.

The ideas presented here are complex. There are some profound, but less complex, ways to consider forgiveness for others, or to find self-forgiveness. Some of these are based in spirituality. One example is the biblical statement "But if ye forgive not men in their transgression neither will your father forgive your transgression" (Matthew 6:15). There are many people who agree with these spiritual ideas; however, the ideas have not yet produced changes in feeling. One barrier to forgiveness may be that forgiveness is not the best thing at a given time; it may not be safe to forgive. I hope that what is offered here may be helpful in considering what forgiveness means and what to do with it.

THE THREE PARTS OF FORGIVENESS

Forgiveness is usually defined as giving up the need to punish or have animosity and anger toward another person. By this definition, forgiveness could be seen as coming in two parts: the punishment and the emotion. As you can see below, a third part has been added.

1. There is the giving up of anger, which can be separate from:
2. Giving up the need to punish, which can be separate from:
3. Redefinition of the relationship.

It is proposed here that forgiveness doesn't have to be complete; you can have partial forgiveness. The parts listed above can be considered separately. You may notice that forgetting has not been mentioned. It may be best to not consider forgetting as part of forgiving. (Maybe this explains the phrase "Forgive AND forget." If forgetting were part of forgiveness, you wouldn't have to mention it.)

What takes the place of anger, punishment, and/or resuming the relationship?

Instead of anger, you might have sadness, compassion, or pity. Instead of punishment, you can have the realization that punishment won't do any good or may hurt you more than the transgressor. Instead of spending time and energy planning or implementing punishment, you can do whatever you like with the time and energy. One thing you cannot have is the exact same relationship, but then change is part of the nature of life. Of course, it is occasionally possible to have complete forgiveness, giving up anger and punishment, and the reconnecting to, perhaps, an even better relationship, but that is not always best or safest.

When you hold back some or all forgiveness, and keep your anger, it may be because you need to be angry to keep yourself from being involved with a person again. When you don't give up punishment, it may be because the punishment is necessary to prevent something from happening again. Before you decide to forgive at all, or how much to forgive, consider these ideas fully.

Do remember that carrying anger, focusing on punishing, and not forgiving may be bad for the person not doing the forgiving. This could be for psychological, social, and/or spiritual reasons. Carrying anger prevents full examination of the factors that led to the transgression, and prevents full understanding how the situation arose, understanding which could prevent future problems. All this is not even to mention that carrying anger can damage our physical health.[22]

APOLOGY

Saying "I'm sorry," the offender's acknowledgement of error and regret, shows that the offender recognizes that he or she took more power than he or she should have. This admission of sorrow demonstrates a willing to display weakness, thereby returning power to the person offended. To give a very mild example, if I bump into you, and then sincerely apologize, I am showing you that you have the power to make me feel bad for what I have done. The balance is restored. Forgiveness can then be offered because you have a signal that you are safe, because hurting you hurts me. While you may not require that I be punished, you may be more careful or less welcoming around me because you now know you have to watch for my clumsiness. On the other hand, you may be more welcoming, and our connection may be better, because you have an example that when I am wrong I will acknowledge it.

Because an apology is supposed to lead to a return of power, an insincere apology can be worse than none. Though the person offering the insincere apology may recognize that he must give up something (the words of apology), he does not have the sadness or the belief in his error to reduce the chance of it recurring.

SELF-FORGIVENESS

The problem of self-forgiveness is especially difficult. In order to begin to consider it, we must recognize that we are complex; we have many parts. When there is self-blame, one part of us is doing the blaming and another part is accused of the transgression,

---

22 Recent research has suggested that successful revenge, as good as it may feel at the moment, sometimes has the result of the revenging person carrying the offense around in a more distressing way than those who don't get revenge.

and in need of forgiveness. When we consider forgiving ourselves, the process becomes easier if the part considering forgiveness has a clear understanding of the part that needs to be forgiven. At different times, two different parts of a person may not forgive each other. For a veteran, sometimes the soldier part may not forgive the civilian part for holding it back in combat; at other times the civilian part may not forgive the soldier part for not holding back. When the two parts of the self can understand each other, we become more unified. Perhaps what people mean when they say they feel "whole" is that their various parts are more connected and understanding.

SELF-FORGIVENESS AND PUNISHMENT

Understanding the nature of punishment is particularly important in self-forgiveness. In psychology, punishment is something that decreases the probability of an event reoccurring. However, most people probably define punishment as inflicting pain, or getting even. When you live in the "get-even" idea of punishment, the chances of the punishment causing more harm than good are high. If you live in the "decrease the chances of re-occurrence" definition, then the punishment chosen will more likely make for a better future. (Punishment for doing wrong is generally, though not always, less effective than reward for doing right. But that is a long discussion for another time.)

In discussing self-forgiveness, it is important to consider that the self-punishment of always feeling guilty — which I define as anger at yourself — usually backfires. People often can take only so much of this before they get angry and turn the blame back on others. An alternative to constant self-blame would be leading your life differently — being more careful, building positive habits. This is usually more difficult for people than feeling bad,[23] which is why people are more likely to punish themselves by feeling bad and screwing up their lives, than to change their habits and forgive themselves. The feeling bad seems to never go away, partly because depriving yourself of pleasure, or hurting

---

23 Part of the difficulty is that people sometimes lose faith that their work toward change will succeed.

yourself, does not usually make things even. It actually makes the situation worse by depriving everyone of your potential to learn from what happened, reconnect, and do good.

RELIGION

Although forgiveness is a major idea in religion, this book cannot explore that connection thoroughly. It might be said, though, that expecting other humans to forgive completely, as we might ask God to do, could be difficult because God, as described by most people, is omnipotent, and cannot be harmed by us. Because of that, God can safely allow the relationship with the transgressor to resume.

WHAT IS LEFT?

We are sometimes faced with a dilemma when we do forgive, and drop the anger or the punishment, but there is no chance for connection or reconnection. If the anger leaves, we may have to accept the loss (and the sadness of it) and the fear of losing our connection to who or what has been lost. In people who have been angry about such a loss, I have observed that when they fully accept the sadness (meaning that they don't beat up on themselves and let the sadness take its course), they find it easier to connect with their positive memories of the person, and the person's value. One common example is after a funeral, when sadness is widely accepted and allowed to take its course, and people may even laugh, remembering and talking about their positive connections to the person who has died. This does not mean that sadness does not come back, only that if it is accepted it doesn't have to stay (see Chapter 4.7).

When anger and grief are overwhelming, it is often helpful to share the accompanying feelings and thoughts with others who might be able to listen compassionately. Many have been there before and found help in a wide variety of places, including from my profession of psychotherapy.

APPENDIX 4:
AN OVERVIEW OF EMDR

THE SHORT VERSION

Eye Movement Desensitization and Reprocessing (EMDR) is a method of psychotherapy developed by Dr. Francine Shapiro in the late 1980s to treat the psychological effects of trauma. Although it contains many components of standard psychotherapy, it initially caused controversy due to its expectation of more rapid results, as well as its use of rapid back-and-forth eye movements (or other sensory/motor activities) led by the therapist. Over time, research has supported the positive results and EMDR has become a method recommended by many professional associations, such as the International Society for Traumatic Stress Studies, and organizations providing mental health care, such as the U.S. Department of Defense and Department of Veterans Affairs.

THE LONGER VERSION

EMDR is a method of psychotherapy developed by psychologist Francine Shapiro as a treatment for psychological distress associated with trauma. She discovered the technique by chance by noticing a decrease in her own emotional distress over a personal concern after having spontaneously moved her eyes back and forth. Integrating her eye movement (EM) observation with aspects of imaginal exposure, cognitive therapy, psychodynamic therapy, and mindfulness teachings, and adding an early positive psychology idea, Shapiro developed a treatment. Following informal tests, Shapiro (1989a) first systematically tested her work in a wait list control study of 21 subjects recruited from local mental health centers, including a Department of Veterans Affairs readjustment center. Remarkably, all of her first 21 subjects showed profound single-session desensitization effects. In addition, Shapiro (1989b) published a case study in a journal edited by Joseph Wolpe, an originator of behavior therapy, in which Wolpe, in an editorial footnote, endorsed Shapiro's technique based on his own informal replication.

In response to Shapiro's unique findings of effectiveness, her attempts to ensure that the method would be taught competently, and the odd nature of the eye movement component, considerable controversy erupted in which academic psychologists, in particular, publicly criticized many aspects of EMDR. Despite this controversial beginning, EMDR has been validated by numerous well-designed outcome studies, which have appeared in scientific peer-reviewed journals. As a result, EMDR has been endorsed as an effective treatment for PTSD by many major U.S. and international evaluating scientific and professional mental health organizations, including the International Society for Traumatic Stress Studies (ISTSS; Foa et. al., 2009), the U.S. Veterans Administration/Department of Defense (2004), the American Psychiatric Association (2004), SAMHSA's National Registry of Evidence-based Programs and Practices (October 2010), and rating bodies in England (Bisson & Andrew, 2007), Northern Ireland (CREST 2003), the Netherlands (Dutch National Steering Committee Guidelines Mental Health Care, 2003), France (INSERM, 2004), and Israel (Bleich et. al., 2002). Other references for the specifics of the research and ratings are available at EMDR.com or EMDRIA.org.

Analogue studies have unequivocally supported the value of the eye movement activity, the most controversial aspect. These studies have demonstrated the role of the eye movement in reducing emotional responsivity and vividness of imagery for emotionally evocative memories (Andrade, Kavanaugh & Baddeley, 1997; Gunter & Bodner, 2008; Kavanagh, Freese, Andrade & May, 2001; Maxfield, Melnyk & Hayman, 2008; Sharpley, Montgomery & Scalzo, 1996; Van den Houts, Muris, Salemink & Kindt, 2001). In clinical dismantling studies, the role of eye movement is supported, but less conclusively (Lipke, 1999). A leading candidate to explain the role of eye movement is the idea that if it takes place while the traumatic memory is brought to "working memory" (Maxfield et. al., 2008), it affects the way that the memory is subsequently stored or reconsolidated.

Along with the positive outcome research, aspects of EMDR that make it a candidate as the first choice of treatment for the psychological effects of trauma are the high frequency of rapid therapeutic effects, the absence of a requirement to disclose the details of the traumatic event or dwell on painful memories, and the absence of a requirement for client homework.

THE BASICS OF EMDR TREATMENT

Shapiro has been careful to distinguish EMDR as a technique from EMDR as a method of treatment or an overall approach to psychotherapy. As a technique for reducing distress related to traumatic incidents, as well as increasing adaptive consideration of these events, clients are asked to bring to awareness a painful image, a related belief about themselves (called the present or negative cognition, e.g. "I am powerless"), and the emotions and body sensations currently associated with this target traumatic event.

Asked to be aware of the preceding, clients are instructed to be mindful of what occurs to them as they follow the therapist's hand with their eyes as it is moved back and forth about a foot and a half in front of the face, across the full range of vision, for about 25 repetitions. The clients, if willing, then report the contents of their awareness at the time the eye movement stopped. (This lack of a requirement to report is one of the attributes that makes EMDR particularly attractive to trauma survivors.) In the most straightforward cases, eye movements are applied to the new contents of awareness and repeated until desensitization or processing is complete. For example, in the middle of a session one might find this interaction:

> Client: *Stupid, that was stupid. I don't see how I ever could have done that.*
>
> Therapist: *See what happens next.* (leads set of EM) *Let it go. Take a deep breath… What comes to you now?*
>
> Client: *Now I am thinking about how I didn't really have a good choice about what to do.*

Therapist: *Notice that.* (leads set of EM) *Take a deep breath…
What comes up now?*

Client: *I'm feeling a little calmer.*

Therapist: *OK, see what happens next.* (leads set of EM)

Before the eye movement activity, clients contemplate the worst
moment of the traumatic event and rate their level of distress on a
0–10 version of Joseph Wolpe's Subjective Units of Disturbance
Scale. Clients are also asked to offer a thought they would prefer
to have when remembering the traumatic event (called the preferred or positive cognition, e.g. "I *do* have choices in life."). The
preferred cognition is rated on a "gut" level of believability from
1 to 7, as the person contemplates the target trauma. These ratings are later used to help evaluate progress toward what Shapiro
first thought of as desensitization, but later considered as reprocessing of the trauma (hence the change of name from the original EMD). If the name were to be reconsidered again, the new
name might take into account the idea that what happens might
best be considered a continuation of processing.

Shapiro (2001) considers EMDR more than the technique described above. As a method of psychotherapy it is described as
including eight phases. The first two encompass common psychotherapy practice (e.g. problem identification, history taking,
evaluation of coping ability, rapport building, explanation of
treatment and stress management). Phases 3 and 4, described
above, are the core of treatment. Phases 5 and 6 involve activities
aimed at making sure reprocessing is complete, that the memory
of the target event is no longer maladaptively distressing, and
if possible, that any good thoughts that can come out of the
event become dominant when the event is contemplated. Phase
7 involves closing a session, especially if the processing is not
complete, and Phase 8 involves re-evaluation of the therapeutic
work in the next session, and finally, termination considerations.
Shapiro says a "three-prong protocol" guides the treatment. This
denotes the need to reprocess memories of past events, present
situations in which the past event leads to maladaptive responses, and imagine possible problematic situations to prepare for
them as they might occur.

THEORETICAL CONSIDERATIONS

As an approach to therapy, Shapiro believes that EMDR contains a philosophy of experience-based psychopathology, embodied by what she currently refers to as the Adaptive Information Processing model (AIP). According to the AIP, experience-based psychopathology is caused by the memory of events being held in dysfunctional "neuro-networks." Natural adaptive information-processing "accommodation and assimilation" have been blocked because of the overwhelming emotion associated with these events.

The reprocessed events need not be what is conventionally called trauma; seemingly innocuous events (an offhand insult at the wrong time, for example) may be taken as traumatic. This recognition of the emotional power of events considered outside of the conventional definition of trauma appears to be consistent with current thinking in the mental health field (see Mol et al., 2005).

As life proceeds, ongoing events trigger these memories, which Shapiro describes as being held in "state-specific" form, producing dysfunctional thoughts, emotions and behavioral responses. This aspect of the AIP has much in common with some earlier theories, including the psychodynamic work on traumatic stress by Mardi Horowitz (1976). The AIP specifies that EMDR treatment is not considered complete until all dysfunctional memories are processed and potential difficult future situations are attended to.

EMDR clinicians have observed that while clients are processing the target memory, other memories with similar themes and sometimes even more emotional power — not necessarily found in the reported history — may arise. They have reported this to be a feature significantly separating the EMDR process from other methods. Documenting the connection of these memories is another key feature of the AIP. In the AIP, traumatic memories are fundamentally, though not exclusively, organized around and connected by their effects.

The feature of the AIP least related to other theory and practice is the expectation that psychotherapeutic response, the reprocessing of memories, can take place very quickly. This is seen in Shapiro's single-session initial studies, as well as in later research, where a one- to three-session psychotherapeutic response is expected in most cases of a single traumatic experience. In contrast, other methods have a longer expected course of treatment, such as the eight to 12 sessions for prolonged exposure, with frequent homework added. This rapid response is attributed to what has so far been referred to, for the sake of clarity, as the eye movement component. In fact, early in the development of EMDR, such activities as alternating bilateral auditory or tactile stimulation were used with clinical success.

The variety of activities that can substitute for eye movement led that aspect of EMDR to be conceptualized and referred to as either bilateral stimulation (BLS) or dual awareness. While each of these attempts to abstractly define this part of therapy capture some aspect of it, all have some theoretical problems. However, other compelling descriptive names have not yet been suggested. If the above-mentioned working memory hypothesis holds up to scrutiny, perhaps the activity will be called the "Working Memory Overload" component. However, this might not explain the research results, which show that eye movement can lead to improved episodic memory, or the above-mentioned tendency of EMDR to bring unexpected new associations, both troubling and redemptive, to awareness. It has been suggested — first by Shapiro, and later in a proposed discussion of possible psycho-physiological mechanisms of effect by neurophysiologist Robert Stickgold (2002) — that the mechanism of effect may be the same as that found in dreaming sleep. REM sleep has been found to produce remote associations. If this is the situation in EMDR, the unexpected troubling associations and "curative" material that come to awareness would be like the "remote" associations not normally accessed during traumatic nightmares and intrusive thoughts and images.

As we can see, while there is plenty of evidence of the psychological effects of eye movement, there are many open questions about the AIP model as the basis of EMDR. The answers as to underlying mechanisms may turn out to be quite complex.

One possible model that would encompass standard EMDR practice, as well as aspects of the AIP, is the Four Activity Model of Psychotherapy Integration (FAM, Lipke, 1999). In this information-processing model, all methods of psychotherapy are seen as having the goal of integrating information to an adaptive resolution, if possible. If not possible, then the goal might be learning to not be overwhelmed by what cannot be so processed. Four activities are employed to accomplish these goals:

1. Accessing of associative networks: Each method of psychotherapy has particular kinds of information it prefers to access (e.g. cognitive therapy tries to access client beliefs about meaning) and particular ways of doing so (e.g. psychoanalysis emphasizes free association). EMDR has direct questions about many aspects of experience: visual images, thoughts, emotions, feeling.

2. Introduction of new information: All methods teach about how psychological problems occur and give the client an understanding that helps set the conditions for information processing.

3. Facilitation of information processing: This is an abstract activity that makes information processing more likely. In EMDR the activity is explicit — eye movement or its substitutes. This model avoids the premature attribution of bilateral stimulation or dual attention to the activity. In other methods, the timing of comments may make it more or less likely that the client makes adaptive connections.

4. Inhibition of information (anxiety) accessing: This refers to the calming exercises provided, which are not directly intended to help information processing (as relaxation would in systematic desensitization) but instead to help the client not be overwhelmed by experience.

EMDR RESEARCH

Following Shapiro's initial controlled study, numerous case studies and then experimental studies appeared. These compared

EMDR with wait list controls and with other methods of treatment for PTSD and acute stress disorder. Subject populations have included children and adults; veterans and civilians; and survivors of natural disasters, sexual abuse, rape, auto accidents, and innumerable other causes of traumatic response. Results have been sustained on follow-up studies of one, three, and 15 months.

There have been several meta-analyses of EMDR effectiveness. When these have compared EMDR with other methods, EMDR has been found to produce results similar to prolonged exposure, the most often highly rated treatment method. Some of these analyses have also supported the rapidity of effectiveness. EMDR efficacy is not likely attributable to researcher allegiance effects, as three controlled EMDR studies conducted by two different respected research teams — two under the leadership of Barbara Rothbaum (1997; et al 2006), a highly regarded exposure treatment advocate — have shown positive results for EMDR despite the fact that the principal investigator would not be considered an EMDR advocate.

Studies have shown EMDR's effectiveness with both acute and chronic traumatic responses. EMDR has also been reported to be used effectively for individuals with diagnoses other than PTSD, including depression, body dysmorphic disorder, chronic pain (including phantom limb pain), phobia, and performance anxiety.

EMDR AND VETERANS

The first published research on EMDR included the presentation of successful treatment with combat veterans as subjects (Shapiro, 1989a). Since then, several other controlled (Carlson et al., 1998) and case studies (Lipke and Botkin, 1999) have been published. Veterans are much more likely to have psychological trauma related to their own actions than civilian trauma survivors. Hence, one aspect of EMDR that makes it particularly valuable in the treatment of combat-related trauma is the way guilt- and shame-based traumatic memories are handled. While cognitive therapy and exposure require discussion of events that the veteran may not be willing to reveal, and exposure therapy is only designed for fear-based trauma, EMDR does not have these limitations. If a client has debilitating PTSD symptoms related to harming or killing, which he fears if revealed might leave him condemned by the therapist, or even in legal jeopardy, work on the most troubling issues, or even therapy itself, may often be avoided. With EMDR the therapist does not need to know the details.

So, in establishing the image, negative cognition, feelings, and an alternative cognition, there can be a general discussion before eye movement begins of how one finds redemption from acts, common in war, that are sometimes called unforgivable. The result of such treatment is that oftentimes, as the eye movement takes place, the veteran comes to understand the necessity of the action and/or the fear or grief behind the action, mourns the loss of those who died and his own loss of innocence, becomes much less likely to have to rely on anger as a defense, and is able to lead a much more productive and less destructive life.

CRITICISMS

Early criticisms of EMDR were strong and sometimes personal, as one might expect of a treatment in which a therapist from California waved her hand in front of the client's face and claimed substantial one-session effects for a problem sometimes considered intractable. The earliest criticisms were based on doubt that the reported outcomes were valid, and that if they were, the therapeutic effects were substantially the result of other established aspects of treatment, especially cognitive therapy and exposure. Ignoring Shapiro's insistence that EMDR be called "experimental" until replications of her research existed, and her promotion of research by offering free training to researchers, another line of criticism (Baer et al., 1992; Herbert et al., 1995) was that the marketing of EMDR included excessive claims, and that the training policies reflected excessive propriety concerns that limited full scientific exploration.

Many of the criticisms have been answered by subsequent research supporting EMDR effectiveness, and in particular the eye movement component of EMDR decreasing the intensity of visual imagery and emotional intensity of memories with a strong affective component. Other research has supported the role of eye movement in promoting intellectual information processing (Christman et al., 2003). Critics have claimed that the EMDR mechanism of effect is simply exposure, or the effects of the protocol's cognitive aspects, but the amount of time dedicated to each of these activities makes this argument problematic. The amount of imaginal exposure is far less than such therapies prescribe, especially when considering that exposure homework is not part of the EMDR protocol, and the client is not encouraged to concentrate on the trauma material, but rather to free-associate to it. A claim that EMDR effects were attributable to mindfulness instructions would be at least as viable as the exposure claim. Similarly, in many EMDR sessions the cognitive restructuring activity is limited to the extent that in those cases it could not account for the level of change observed clinically or in experimental studies.

An independent professional association, the EMDR International Association (EMDRIA), has been established to oversee training, helping to address the question of Shapiro's proprietary control; however, criticism remains. Sometimes this is from advocates of EMDR who object to what they consider excessive control over the content and form of training requirements, as well as requirements to establish and maintain the various levels of "expertise" mandated by the organization.

In addition, Shapiro's AIP model has been elevated to being the foundational model of EMDR, and is now sometimes described as inextricable from it. There is value in the AIP's description of how psychological problems can be corrected, and personal growth promoted. However, there are other aspects of the AIP that leave it less effective as a theory than EMDR is as a therapy. One of these problems is that while, as mentioned above, in many cases cognitive restructuring is very limited and could not account for the observed level of therapeutic change, in a minority of cases there is a strong reliance on the kind of cognitive or interpretive interventions found in other traditions of psychotherapy. The AIP does not account for the cognitive restructuring that is part of the method as it is taught and practiced.

Current representations of the AIP (e.g. Solomon and Shapiro, 2008) fail to conceptualize this integration of mechanisms of effect. Another limitation of the AIP is the premature reliance on psycho-physiological terminology and conceptualization (Lipke, 2009). If EMDR can be considered from other points of view, such as the FAM discussed above, it may find more acceptance in academic circles.

CURRENT STATUS

While EMDR is widely accepted as an evidence-based treatment for PTSD and is used extensively (based on reports from various EMDR training organizations, it is reasonable to say that more than 100,000 therapists have been trained worldwide), it has not found a comfortable home in the academic world in the U.S. Two reasons for this may be that most of the early strong criticism of EMDR came from established academics who find it difficult to accept research results that contradict their earlier opinions, and that EMDRIA has not established training policies that promote the academic freedom expected in the university. Nonetheless, research activity on EMDR is extensive and continually growing. Studies, many of them from research groups outside the United States, cover mechanisms of effect and explore EMDR's potential with problems and concerns beyond PTSD. Since 2007 there has been a peer-reviewed journal, the *Journal of EMDR Practice and Research*, dedicated to research and clinical reports on EMDR. At least as much as with any other subject, in order to be up to date with the current status of EMDR, one must follow the journals or proceedings of professional conferences.

APPENDIX 5:
FIGHTING THE LAST WAR: COURAGE AND WISDOM

This appendix comes out of discussions of issues addressed in meetings with combat veterans in the Stress Disorder Treatment Unit at North Chicago VAMC (now Lovell Federal Health Care Center).

THE SHORTER VERSION

In combat, the main psychological challenge is to, minute by minute, find courage to overcome fear and pain. That is the goal of most military training. The main challenge of civilian life, however, is to find wisdom to define and meet long-term goals. Knowing this is a big step toward overcoming the problems that come with mistaking civilian challenges for combat challenges.

THE LONGER VERSION

When a war is not won, it is sometimes said of the strategist and commanders that they were fighting the last war — that is, the previous war. There is some truth to this, not only in the business of war, but for life in general. All of us try to be on guard to prevent recurrences of past problems, applying the lessons of the past. While this is often sensible, it may distract from some aspects of current threats and the different solutions they require. For combat veterans, paying excess attention to the past can be more of a problem than for other people. Because the severity and intensity of the past threat are so profound, so much about life and death, and the resulting habits are so ingrained, current civilian threats are sometimes reacted to as if they were the old combat problems, which can lead to dangerously destructive, and regretted, actions.

The psychological problem of war is very much that of finding courage to control fear and pain in combat. Most people have to change profoundly to do this. When people who have been through such experiences return to less physically dangerous and challenging civilian life, they are in danger of continuing to act as if finding or maintaining physical courage is the challenge, so they sometimes maintain combat behavior to face this challenge. This can be through avoidance of risks (which can mean avoiding people in general) or embracing risks to maintain their "edge." However, physical courage is not the primary challenge in civilian life. In civilian life, the greatest challenge is finding wisdom.

One aspect of this problem is that the courage challenge is ingrained both by military training and experience. Another is that after combat, veterans need to show great wisdom as they face memories of horrors of life that most people never encounter, as well as the deaths of loved ones, physical impairment, and other losses that most people don't face until they're older, when they've had more time to make sense out of their experiences.

Below is an example of a situation encountered by two veterans, followed by a discussion of the relationship between understanding the world primarily as a test of courage versus as a test of wisdom.

A Vietnam War veteran — let's call him Bob — and a veteran of the Persian Gulf wars, Leo, took a trip to a grand museum. Bob was wearing gear that identified him as a Vietnam War veteran. Some fool approached them and began to insult Bob about the outcome of the war. Leo was even more outraged than Bob, and had to be restrained from physically attacking the fool. Amazingly, the fool returned, resumed his insults, and then ran away. Leo headed off trying to find him to do something that would lead to much greater and more regrettable problems than enduring the insult, as emotionally painful as that was. Fortunately, as he could later acknowledge, Leo didn't find him. That was the story told in our group discussion on the Monday following the event.

Here is the analysis that came out of the group discussion:

1. Wisdom requires consideration of long-term goals, benefits, and costs. Wisdom does not just mean putting up with stuff, and/or running away. Discretion is not the better part of valor; it is the better part of wisdom.[24] Perhaps, one way to make the relationship clearer is that in the military, in combat, you have already made the decision to follow orders, so the test is whether or not you can find the courage to do so. In civilian life, you have to continually decide what does and doesn't make sense. I am aware that this is not an all-or-nothing proposition. Sometimes wisdom must be shown in combat and sometimes courage, even physical courage, must be shown in civilian life. What we are addressing here is the general situation, not every possible example.

2. Some readers will be familiar with the Reinhold Niebuhr serenity prayer,[25] which posits that wisdom is knowing the difference between when courage is required and when acceptance is required. While the serenity prayer can be profoundly useful, this situation requires more than a decision between traditionally defined courage to change the situation or acceptance that the painful insult must be passively accepted. What is needed is a rethinking of the situation so that it is between other choices.

3. Here is one possible rethinking of Leo's reaction. If this is a test of Leo's courage, that means the insult is an attack, similar to an attack in war, and his buddy must be defended to the death. But wisdom may tell us that this is not war, and the insult is probably either the prattling of a fool or the anger of a person

---

24 When Shakespeare wrote "The better part of valor is discretion..." (Henry IV Part I, Act V, Sc. 4) he put it in the mouth of his great coward, Falstaff.

25 The original version, according to Elisabeth Sifton (2003), daughter of the author, Reinhold Niebuhr, states: "God, give us grace to accept with serenity the things that cannot be changed, courage to change the things that should be changed, and the wisdom to distinguish the one from the other." (p. 277) This is slightly different from the version used by Alcoholics Anonymous to give so much inspiration to so many.

so profoundly injured himself that he needs to try
to hurt someone else to divert himself from his own
pain. If this is the case, what is the best response to
the fool? What is the goal? If it is to change him so
he doesn't do it again, then perhaps a beating will
do that. If so, is it worth it? Is it worth accidentally
killing him? Is it worth going to jail? Is the goal to
have the buddy's feelings protected? Will attacking
the fool and going to jail leave the buddy more comforted or less comforted? What does your wisdom
say?

A FAMOUS WARRIOR'S EXAMPLE

Of course, combat isn't purely about physical courage, nor is
civilian life purely about wisdom. The following passage is from
Soldier's Heart, by Elizabeth D. Samet (2007), a book describing
her experience teaching literature at West Point. It shows how
deeply ingrained the question of physical courage is in soldiers.
Samet quotes and comments on a passage from the memoirs
of Ulysses S. Grant (1885/1999). It should be mentioned that
Grant had, in previous combat, already displayed exemplary
physical courage. It would have seemed that he no longer needed
to pass the test. Nonetheless:

At the beginning of the Civil War, however, Grant had his first
real command, and he lacked a knowledge and maturity com-
mensurate with his newly increased responsibilities. Tracking
Colonel Thomas Harris in the vicinity of Florida, Mo., he faced
and failed one of his first tests of combat leadership:

> *As we approached the brow of the hill from which it was
> expected we could see Harris' camp, and possible face his
> men ready formed to meet us, my heart kept getting high-
> er and higher until it felt to me as though it was in my
> throat. I would have given anything to be back in Illinois
> but I had not the moral courage to halt and consider what
> to do; I kept right on. When we reached a point from
> which the valley below was in full view I halted. The*

place from where Harris had been encamped a few days before was still there and the marks of a recent encampment were plainly visible, but the troops were gone. My heart resumed its place. It occurred to me at once that Harris had been as much afraid of me as I had been of him. This view of the question I had never taken before; but it was one I never forgot afterward.

In this passage and in the episodes that follow, one can see the unknown become known, and the terror subsiding, as Grant realizes that he and his enemy shared the very same fears. Yet it is important to note that it was not the enemy, but his own men, who frightened Grant at this stage. His admission, "I had not the moral courage to halt," suggests that he was worried as a new commander that his men would think him a physical coward.

Grant was not moving from combat to civilian life, but rather to the challenges of command. However, he still had to go from the challenge of physical courage to that of what we have here been calling wisdom, as he moved into command. In his memoirs, Grant reports that he learned from this experience. May we all.

APPENDIX 6:
DREAMS AND TRAUMA

"...there is nothing either good or bad but thinking makes it so... Oh God! I could be bounded in a nutshell and count myself a king of infinite space, were it not that I have bad dreams." — Hamlet, Act II, Sc. 2 [26]

The waking mind and sleeping mind work by different sets of rules. Each can help the other, or cause difficulty. The waking mind's most common complaint about the sleeping mind is the presence of nightmares.

One way to decrease nightmares and the emotional distress related to them is to understand the purpose of dreams in general. There are lots of theories about dreams, and the following is a combination of different theories and observations in the field of psychology, as well as what I have learned from my own observations, and especially from asking my clients, mostly combat veterans, about their dreams and nightmares.

Like our waking mind, our sleeping/dreaming mind seems to have several different functions. For the sleeping mind these include:

1. Consolidating learning: Research shows that sleep after learning something new can improve our long-term memory of it.

2. Wish fulfillment: Our dreams sometimes give us kinds of enjoyment we are not able to attain in waking life. I probably don't need to give examples.

3. Problem solving: The following are related, but may be considered separately:

   a. Intellectual problems: There is a famous example in which a scientist, Otto Loewi, in 1936, won a Nobel Prize after dreaming of the answer to a problem about neurotransmitters (Hobson,

---

26 I know I used this earlier in the book, but it is so good, I wanted to use it again.

1988). He dreamt about a snake shaped like the molecule he was trying to describe, demonstrating that the dreaming brain usually works in pictures rather than words.

b. Emotion problems: The dreaming mind presents us with our worst fears, including replays of horrible events from the past, usually in movielike form. With past traumatic events, it seems as if the dream is trying to get the event to come out differently. The dreaming mind is very smart about some things, but it doesn't know the past can't be changed; in fact, it doesn't know the past from the present. It thinks everything is in the present. So it thinks it can still change past events. When fears or worries of the future are dreamt of, we may be getting a chance to prepare in case the worst happens. Often people feel guilty because they have a bizarre and frightening dream. They may believe the wish fulfillment theory, about how they really wish for this horrible thing, applies. That does not appear to make sense in this situation, given everything else we know about dreams and about how people do overcome the distress of nightmares. It makes about as much sense as thinking people go to zombie movies because their deepest and most sincere desire is to have their brains eaten. When people wake up during a nightmare, it is probably because the emotional pain is so great that it overrides the part of the brain that is keeping the person asleep. It is like the mind has pushed an eject button to exit from the dream.

4. To keep us asleep: Sometimes the sleeping mind will create a dream story that includes some aspect of a real situation. The mind seemingly makes up a dream around this event to explain what is happening, allowing the person to keep sleeping. For example, if a siren goes off outside the sleeper's window, the dream story might include a loud noise.

What to do about nightmares:

1. Understand the nature of the dream world.

    a. Recognize the purposes of dreams, as described above.

    b. Recognize that our dreaming mind operates by different rules than our waking mind. The dreaming mind emphasizes pictures. It doesn't know that there is a past; everything is in the present. It doesn't obey rules of physics (people can fly, etc.). Dreams usually are not remembered unless we wake up during them or just after they occur, and they tend to be forgotten quickly, unless they are very traumatic.

    c. Recognize that dreams and nightmares about real events may change over time. Sometimes this is part of an event becoming less destructively painful. Sometimes changes of places and people (a family member is now in the combat zone, for example) don't bring a lowering of painful emotion because the changed situation is still a strong signal for fear.

2. Do EMDR work with a therapist on the situations that are connected to the dreams.

3. Do work with a therapist to directly affect the dream content. In one method of therapy, developed by Barry Krakow, Image Rehearsal Therapy (IRT, Moore & Krakow, 2010), a new ending is made up for the dream/nightmare. The person starts at the start of the nightmare and then makes up a story, in movie form, of what he or she would like to see happen. There are no rules; any kind of strange thing might happen. Sometimes people resist this because they think that it is not facing the truth. They forget that the dream is always false in the sense that the person is reliving the event as if it is still happening, when in fact it is not. The dreaming mind would have come to its own "magic" solution if sleep had continued; however, since the eject button was pushed, and the person woke up, it is up to the waking mind

to come to the magic solution. This technique often works. The result is not that the event is forgotten, just that it is not repeated in nightmares, and it is remembered as an event, and not relived, when it is thought about. In addition, when even the most horrible events from the past are remembered instead of relived, then any worthwhile elements they have can be appreciated. For example, if someone died as a result of the event, it allows us to remember why we cared about them, allowing them to stay with us in a positive way, rather than us just remembering the pain of their death.

APPENDIX 7:
A QUICK GUIDE TO HEART

1. HEArt is an activity to practice if your goal is to reduce anger — not all anger, only anger you find destructive. However, it is about more than just anger; it is about the ability to recognize your emotions when it is safe to do so. It is also about more than just managing anger; it is about making it so that, sometimes, anger doesn't even begin, and therefore doesn't need to be managed.

2. The discussion of emotion and feeling here is based on scientific and philosophical understanding, input from veterans, and the author's own experience. It should be noted that there is disagreement among psychologists in the understanding of emotion, and all will not agree with these definitions.

3. When demonstrating and helping others to practice HEArt, the most important principle is that emotions/feelings in the anger family are there to push things away, including other, more painful emotions. Anger is often present, even when it is self-destructive, because of the power one feels with it.

4. The emotions most likely being pushed away — that is, being kept from becoming feelings or staying that way — are in the sadness, fear, and happiness/love families of emotion.

5. Sadness is an emotion about past loss, fear is about future loss, and love is about gaining connection. Unless there is some threat of loss or pain, it usually doesn't make sense to push something away.

6. If these emotions can be named, even if not completely felt, the anger doesn't have much of a job, so it will either not appear, or be weaker and less destructive.

7. In order to name the emotions,[27] or allow them to be experienced, there must be a way to make it so they do not become intolerably destructive. The things that can help with this are:

  - Spiritual and philosophical beliefs.

  - Learning to not fight them, but keeping behavior calm until they decrease, which they naturally do (even if they may come back later).

  - Talking with someone about them:

    ◦ For fear-based emotions, by using the fear to figure out how real the threat is, and how to protect yourself.

    ◦ For sadness, knowing the loss that caused the sadness, which helps to clarify what was not lost.

8. Humor, a combination of direct feeling change and cognitive insight.

9. Part of what makes the sadness and fear family emotions so painful in current situations is that they lead people to relive past grief and terror. So making peace with the past is an important part of preventing destructive anger. However, intensive therapy, in addition to HEArt, is often the best way to accomplish this.

10. HEArt is not always the best way to address anger. Sometimes, just getting away from the situation, using relaxation or meditation to calm down, or thinking about things logically is best. This is especially true after anger has started to increase.

11. A good way to learn HEArt is to practice identifying/naming emotions in the fear or sadness families before you get into situations in which they might be blocked by anger. Another is to look back at times in which destructive anger — anger you regret — arose, and then identify the hidden emotions that anger blocked from becoming feelings.

---

27 This simply means just saying the word, for example "I have fear," or "sadness." If you know it must be there, even if you don't feel it.

12. Positive emotions in the happiness/love families of emotion are sometimes blocked by anger because people fear that connecting to others increases the chance of pain in the future. Acknowledging the more positive emotions is usually more difficult than the painful emotions.

13. Though not an emotion, physical pain is often also blocked by anger.

14. In some ways destructive anger is like alcohol or drug abuse, problem gambling, or other destructive habits.

15. "What's sauce for the goose is sauce for the gander." If your anger rises to block your pain, then the same thing is true of others.

16. HEArt stands for **H**idden **E**motion **Art**iculation, meaning the naming of hidden emotions.

APPENDIX 8:
A QUICKER GUIDE TO HEART

1. Sometimes anger comes up to block us from sadness and/or fear.

2. If we acknowledge fear and/or sadness, there is less anger because it doesn't have a job.

3. People tend to believe this doesn't work because that is part of how sadness and fear are hidden, or because they are too smart to fall for a psychologist's tricks. As always, you decide.

APPENDIX 9:
A MARTIAL ARTS PERSPECTIVE

Many readers of this book will have been raised to think that fear and other painful emotions are signs of weakness, and must always be fought and blocked. Destructive anger can be a weapon for those people in the fight against fear and pain, but when that weapon turns back on them, it can become more destructive than the fear would be. The destructive anger becomes a traitor.

Here, again, are the levels of the HEArt program, but seen through this fighting perspective. In this language of fighting, the opponent is not the person who made you angry, but rather the destructive anger itself.

I. Physical Presence

This is the strategy to employ when an opponent is overwhelming. We are not talking about David and Goliath; we are talking about a charging rhino, and you don't even have a slingshot. So when you are in, or might be going to, a situation where you likely won't be able to fight off your dangerous, destructive anger and violence, the advice here is to get away, or to not get into the situation at all.

II. and III. Physiological Control and Thinking Rationally

These skill levels are combined because both are direct attacks on destructive anger. These skills are comparable to striking, or blocking and striking. One skill attacks the physiology of anger, the biological arousal, by employing calming or meditation techniques. The other attacks the thought processes of anger, refuting illogical ideas that promote the destructive, angry behavior.

IV. Identifying Underlying Emotion

The HEArt program calls for us to invite in the emotions underlying the anger, rendering the anger useless as a defense against them. This is comparable to moves in martial arts in which the energy of the attack is brought in and then reversed. It is argued here that bringing in the painful emotion is no more a sign of weakness than is bringing in an opponent's attack to flip him off his feet, as one might see in judo. Perhaps the most famous extended example of this is Muhammad Ali's so-called "rope-a-dope" fighting style against George Foreman. I am not saying that bringing in an emotion will be painless, only that in the end it might be the best way to not be destroyed by anger, and the most sophisticated fighting technique available against destructive anger.

REFERENCES

Achebe, Chinua (1959). *Things Fall Apart*. Anchor Books.

American Psychiatric Association (2004). Practice Guideline for the Treatment of Patients with Acute Stress Disorder and Posttraumatic Stress Disorder. Arlington, Va.: American Psychiatric Association Practice Guidelines.

Asmundson, G.J.G.; Stapleton, J.A. & Taylor, Steven (2006). Are avoidance and numbing distinct PTSD symptom clusters? *Journal of Traumatic Stress* (17), pp. 467-475.

Baer, L.; Hurley, J.D.; Minichiello, W.E.; Ott, B.D.; Penzel, F. & Ricciardi, J. (1992). EMDR workshop: Disturbing issues? *The Behavior Therapist*, 15, pp. 110–111.

Banks, Russell (1991). *The Sweet Hereafter*. New York: Harper.

Barr-Zisowicz, C. (2000). "Sadness" – Is there such a thing? In: Lewis, M. & Haviland-Jones (Eds.) *Handbook of Emotions (second edition)*, pp. 607–622. New York: Guilford.

Bisson, J. & Andrew, M. (2007). Psychological treatment of post-traumatic stress disorder (PTSD). *Cochrane Database of Systematic Reviews* 2007, Issue 3. Art. No.: CD003388. DOI: 10.1002/14651858.CD003388.pub3.

Bleich, A.; Kotler, M.; Kutz, I. & Shalev, A. (2002). A position paper of the (Israeli) National Council for Mental Health: Guidelines for the assessment and professional intervention with terror victims in the hospital and in the community. Jerusalem, Israel.

Carlson, J.G.; Chemtob, C.; Rusnak, K.; Hedlund, N. & Muraoka, M. (1998) Eye Movement Desensitization and Reprocessing (EMDR) treatment for combat-related posttraumatic stress disorder. *Journal of Traumatic Stress*, 11, pp. 3–24.

Christman, S.D.; Garvey, K.J.; Propper, R.E. & Phaneuf, K.A. (2003). Bilateral eye movements enhance the retrieval of episodic memories. *Neuropsychology*, 17, pp. 221–229.

CREST (2003). The management of posttraumatic stress disorder in adults. A publication of the Clinical Resource Efficiency Support Team of the Northern Ireland Department of Health, Social Services and Public Safety, Belfast.

Curtis, M.E. & Bharucha, J.J. (2010). The minor third communicates sadness in speech, mirroring its use in music. *Emotion*, 10, pp. 335–348.

Damasio, A. (1999). *The Feeling of What Happens*. San Diego: Harcourt.

Damasio, A. (2003). *Looking for Spinoza*. Orlando: Harcourt.

Department of Veterans Affairs & Department of Defense (2004). VA/DoD Clinical Practice Guideline for the Management of Post-Traumatic Stress. Washington, D.C.: Veterans Health Administration, Department of Veterans Affairs and Health Affairs, Department of Defense. Office of Quality and Performance publication 10Q-CPG/PTSD-04.

Dollard, J. & Miller, N.E. (1950). *Personality and Psychotherapy*. New York: McGraw-Hill.

Dutch National Steering Committee Guidelines Mental Health Care (2003). Multidisciplinary Guideline Anxiety Disorders. Quality Institute Health Care CBO/Trimbos Institute. Utrecht, Netherlands.

Ellis, Albert (1995). Rational Emotive Behavior Therapy. In: Corsini, R.J. & Wedding, D. *Current Psychotherapies* Itasca, IL, F.E. Peacock, pp. 162–196.

Filkins, Dexter (12/21/04). *All Things Considered*, NPR.

Foa, E.B.; Keane, T.M.; Friedman, M.J. & Cohen, J.A. (2009). Effective treatments for PTSD: Practice Guidelines of the International Society for Traumatic Stress Studies (2nd ed.). New York: Guilford Press.

Frank, J.D. & Frank, J.B. (1991). *Persuasion and Healing: A Comparative Study of Psychotherapy (third edition)*. Baltimore: Johns Hopkins University Press.

Frijda, N. (1988). The laws of emotion. *American Psychologist*, 43, pp. 349–358.

Goleman, Daniel (1995). *Emotional Intelligence*. New York: Bantam.

Gottman, J.M. & Silver, Nan (1999). *The Seven Principles for Making Marriage Work*. New York: Three Rivers Press.

Grant, U.S. (1885/1999). *Personal Memoirs*. New York: Penguin.

Gray, Jeffrey Alan (1987). *The Psychology of Fear and Stress* (second edition). New York: Cambridge University Press.

Herbert, J.D.; Lilienfeld, S.; Lohr, J.; Montgomery, R.W.; O'Donohue, W.; Rosen, G.M. & Tolin, D. (2000). Science and pseudoscience in the development of Eye Movement Desensitization and Reprocessing: Implications for clinical psychology. *Clinical Psychology Review*, 20, pp. 945–971.

Hobson, J. A. (1988). The Dreaming Brain. New York: Basic Books.

Horowitz, Mardi (1976). *Stress Response Syndromes*. New York: Jason Aronson.

INSERM (2004). Psychotherapy: An evaluation of three approaches. French National Institute of Health and Medical Research, Paris, France.

Ironson, G.I.; Freund, B.; Strauss, J.L. & Williams, J. (2002). Comparison of two treatments for traumatic stress: A community-based study of EMDR and prolonged exposure. *Journal of Clinical Psychology*, 58, pp. 113–128.

Janoff-Bulman, R. (1992). *Shattered Assumptions: Toward a New Psychology of Trauma*. New York: The Free Press.

Kahneman, D.; Knetsch, J.L. & Thaler, R. H. (1986). Fairness and the assumptions of economics. *Journal of Business*, 59, S285–S300.

King, L.A.; King, D.W.; Orazem, R.J. & Palmieri, P.A. (2006). Research on the latent structure of PTSD. *PTSD Research Quarterly*. Summer, pp. 1–7.

Kubler-Ross, E. (1970). *On Death and Dying.* New York: MacMillan.

Lewis, C.S. (1961, 1994). *A Grief Observed.* Harper San Francisco.

Lewis, Michael (2000). The emergence of human emotions. In: Lewis, M. & Haviland-Jones (Eds.) *Handbook of Emotions (second edition),* pp. 265–280. New York: Guilford.

Lewis, Michael & Jones, J.M.H., *Handbook of Emotions* (second edition). New York: Guilford.

Lieberman, Matthew D. (2011). Why symbolic processing of affect can disrupt negative affect: Social cognitive and affective neuroscience investigations. In: Todorov, A.; Fiske, S. T. & Prentice, D., *Social Neuroscience: Toward Understanding the Underpinnings of the Social Mind.* Oxford University Press.

Lieberman, M.D.; Eisenberger, N.I.; Crockett, M.J.; Tom, S.M.; Pfeifer, J.H. & Way, Baldwin (published online 6/15/07). Putting feelings into words: Affect labeling disrupts amygdala activity in response to affective stimuli. *Psychological Science,* 15, pp. 421–428.

Lipke, H.J. (1999). EMDR and Psychotherapy Integration. Boca Raton: CRC Press.

Lipke, H.J. (2009) Letter to the editor: On science, orthodoxy, EMDR and the AIP. *Journal of EMDR Practice and Research,* pp. 109–110.

Lipke, H.J. and Botkin A. (1993). Case studies of Eye Movement Desensitization and Reprocessing (EMDR) with chronic post-traumatic stress disorder. *Psychotherapy,* 29:4, pp. 591–595.

Lutz, Tom (1999). *Crying,* New York: Norton.

Maciejewski, P.K.; Zhang, B.; Block, S.D. & Prigerson, H.G. (2007). *Journal of the American Medical Association,* 297(7), pp. 716–722.

Maher, Brendan (1969). *Clinical Psychology and Personality: The Selected Papers of George Kelly.* New York: Wiley.

Maxfield, Louise; Melnyk, W.T. & Hayman, C.A. Gordon (2008). A working memory explanation for the effects of eye movement in EMDR. *Journal of EMDR Practice and Research*, pp. 247–268.

Milton, John (1999). *The Annotated Milton: Paradise Lost*, New York: Bantan.

Mol, S.S.L.; Arntz, A.; Metsemakers, J.F.M.; Dinant, G.; Montfort, P.A.V. & Knottnerus, J.A. (2005). Symptoms of post-traumatic stress disorder after non-traumatic events: Evidence from an open population study. *British Journal of Psychiatry*, 186, pp. 494–499.

Moore, Bret A. & Krakow, Barry (2010). Imagery rehearsal therapy: An emerging treatment for posttraumatic nightmares in veterans. *Psychological Trauma: Theory, Research, Practice, and Policy*, 2(3), pp. 232–238.

Morgan, Hillary J. & Janoff-Bulman (1994). Positive and negative self-complexity: Patterns of adjustment following traumatic versus non-traumatic life experiences. *Journal of Social and Clinical Psychology*, 13, pp. 63–85.

Novaco, R.W. & Chemtob, C.M. (2002). Anger and combat-related posttraumatic stress disorder. *Journal of Traumatic Stress*, 15, pp. 123–132.

Panksapp, Jann (1998). *Affective Neuroscience: The Foundations of Human and Animal Emotions*. New York: Oxford University Press.

Rhodes, Richard (1999). *Why They Kill*. New York: Vintage.

Robinson, J.A. & Swanson, K.L. (1993). Field and observer modes of remembering. *Memory* 1(3), pp. 169–184.

Ross, L. & Nisbett, R.E. (1991). *The Person and the Situation*. New York: McGraw-Hill.

Rothbaum, B.; Astin, M. & Marsteller, F. (2006). Prolonged exposure versus Eye Movement Desensitization and Reprocessing (EMDR) for PTSD rape victims. *Journal of Traumatic Stress*, 18, pp. 607–616.

Rothbaum, Barbara (1997). A controlled study of Eye Movement Desensitization and Reprocessing in the treatment of posttraumatic stress disordered victims. *Bulletin of the Menninger Clinic*, 61, pp. 317–334.

Samet, E.D. (2007). *Soldier's Heart*. New York: Picador.

SAMHSA's National Registry of Evidence-based Programs and Practices (October 2010). Eye Movement Desensitization and Reprocessing. http://nrepp.samhsa.gov/ViewIntervention. aspx?id=199

Schneider, Jens; Hofman, Arne; Rost, Christin & Shapiro, Francine (2008). EMDR in the Treatment of Chronic Phantom Limb Pain. *Pain Medicine*, 9, pp. 76–82.

Servan-Schreiber, D. (2003). *The Instinct to Heal*. Rodale.

Severo, Richard, and Milford, Lewis (1989). *The Wages of War* New York: Simon and Schuster.

Shapiro, F. (2001). *Eye Movement Desensitization and Reprocessing: Basic Principles, Protocols and Procedures* (2nd ed.). New York: Guilford.

Shapiro, Francine (1989a). Efficacy of the Eye Movement Desensitization Procedure in the treatment of traumatic memories. *Journal of Traumatic Stress*. 2(2), pp. 199–223.

Shapiro, Francine (1989b). Eye Movement Desensitization: A new treatment of post-traumatic stress disorder. *Journal of Behavior Therapy and Experimental Psychiatry*. 20(3), pp. 211–217.

Sherman, R.A. (in collaboration with, Devor, M.; Jones, D.E.C.; Katz, J. & Marbach, J.J.) 1996. *Phantom Pain*. New York: Plenum.

Sifton, Elisabeth (2003). *The Serenity Prayer*. New York: Norton.

Solomon, R.M. & Shapiro, Francine (2008). EMDR and the Adaptive Information Processing model, pp. 315–325.

Spates, C.R.; Koch, E.; Cusak, K.; Pagato, S. & Waller, S. (2009). Eye Movement Desensitization and Reprocessing. In Foa, E.B.; Keane, T.M.; Friedman, M.J. & Cohen, J.A. *Effective treatments for PTSD: Practice Guidelines of the International Society for Traumatic Stress Studies* (2nd ed.) New York: Guilford Press.

Stickgold, Robert (2002). EMDR: A putative neurobiological mechanism of action. *Journal of Clinical Psychology*, 58, pp. 61–76.

Sullivan, H.S. (1954). *The Psychiatric Interview*. New York: Norton.

Tangney, J.P. & Dearing, R.L. (2002). *Shame and Guilt*. New York: Guilford.

Tavris, Carol (1989). *Anger: the Misunderstood Emotion,* revised edition. New York: Simon & Schuster.

Van Etten, M. & Taylor, Steven (1998). Comparative efficacy of treatments for post-traumatic stress disorder: A meta-analysis. *Clinical Psychology and Psychotherapy*, 5, pp. 126–144.

Wilson, S.; Becker, L.A. & Tinker, R.H. (1997). Fifteen-month follow-up of eye movement desensitization and reprocessing (EMDR) treatment of post-traumatic stress disorder and psychological trauma. *Journal of Consulting and Clinical Psychology*, 65, pp. 1047–1056.

Zajonc, R.B. (1984). On the primacy of affect. *American Psychologist*, 39, pp. 117–123.

ABOUT THE AUTHOR

Howard Lipke, Ph.D., is a clinical psychologist who has provided psychotherapeutic services to combat veterans for more than 35 years. He has also taught and trained fellow mental health professionals for much of that time. He is a former director of the residential PTSD treatment program, and the team leader of the outpatient PTSD program, at what is now the Lovell Federal Health Care Center. Among other publications, he has authored the book *EMDR and Psychotherapy Integration*, co-authored a chapter in Moore and Penk's *Treating PTSD in Military Personnel*, and written and co-authored several professional journal articles. He is the co-editor of the column *Trauma and World Literature* in the International Society for Traumatic Stress Studies' newsletter *Traumatic StressPoints*, and is on the editorial board of the *Journal of EMDR Practice and Research*.

Dr. Lipke has provided pro bono direct service for survivors, and training for treating clinicians, related to such events as the Oklahoma City bombing, the World Trade Center attack, and ongoing crises in Bangladesh and Israel. He was trained in group psychotherapy by Irvin Yalom, Critical Incident Stress Debriefing by Jeffrey Mitchell, and neuropsychological testing by Ralph Reitan.

Dr. Lipke is on the clinical faculty at the Rosalind Franklin University of Health Science. Since retiring from the VA he continues to write, consult, and provide some direct service to veterans and training to their psychotherapists.

Photo: Michael L. Abramson

CPSIA information can be obtained at www.ICGtesting.com
Printed in the USA
BVOW04s1709041113

335335BV00006B/37/P